European Administrative Governance Series

Series Editors
Thomas Christiansen, Professor of European Institutional Politics, Department of Political Science, Maastricht University, The Netherlands

Sophie Vanhoonacker, Professor of Administrative Governance, Department of Political Science, Maastricht University, The Netherlands

The series maps the range of disciplines addressing the study of European public administration. In particular, contributions to the series will engage with the role and nature of the evolving bureaucratic processes of the European Union, including the study of the EU's civil service, of organizational aspects of individual institutions such as the European Commission, the Council of Ministers, the External Action Service, the European Parliament, the European Court and the European Central Bank, and of inter-institutional relations among these and other actors. The series also welcomes contributions on the growing role of EU agencies, networks of technical experts and national officials, and of the administrative dimension of multi-level governance, including international organizations. Of particular interest in this respect will be the emergence of a European diplomatic service and the management of the EU's expanding commercial, foreign, development, security and defence policies, as well as the role of institutions in a range of other policy areas of the Union.

Beyond this strong focus of EU administrative governance, the series will also include texts on the development and practice of administrative governance within European states. This may include contributions to the administrative history of Europe, which is not simply about rules and regulations governing bureaucracies, or about formal criteria for measuring the growth of bureaucracies but, rather, about the concrete workings of public administration, both in its executive functions and in its involvement in policy-making. Furthermore, the series will include studies on the interaction between the national and European levels, with particular attention paid to the impact of the EU on domestic administrative systems.

Titles include:

Tannelie Blom and Sophie Vanhoonacker (*editors*)
THE POLITICS OF INFORMATION
The Case of the European Union

Hylke Dijkstra
POLICY-MAKING IN EU SECURITY AND DEFENCE
An Institutional Perspective

Didier Georgakakis and Jay Rowell (*editors*)
THE FIELD OF EUROCRACY
Mapping EU Actors and Professionals

Anna-Lena Högenauer, Christine Neuhold and Thomas Christiansen
PARLIAMENTARY ADMINISTRATIONS IN THE EUROPEAN UNION

Aneta Spendzharova
REGULATING BANKS IN CENTRAL AND EASTERN EUROPE
Through Crisis and Boom

European Administrative Governance Series
Series Standing Order ISBN 978–1–137–29475–3 (paperback)
and 978–0–230–35976–5 (cased)
(*outside North America only*)

You can receive future titles in this series as they are published by placing a standing order. Please contact your bookseller or, in case of difficulty, write to us at the address below with your name and address, the title of the series and the ISBNs quoted above.

Customer Services Department, Macmillan Distribution Ltd, Houndmills, Basingstoke, Hampshire RG21 6XS, England

---

Contents

Tables and Figures

Tables

Figures

Acknowledgements

We would like to thank the Nederlandse Organisatie voor Wetenschappelijk Onderzoek, the Dutch research council, for financing the research that led to this book (Grant no. 464–10-074).

Special thanks also go to our OPAL partners at the University of Cambridge (Julie Smith, Geoffrey Edwards and Ariella Huff), at the University of Cologne (Wolfgang Wessels, Katjana Gattermann, Oliver Höing and Claudia Hefftler) and at the Institut d'Etudes Politiques in Paris (Olivier Rozenberg, Katrin Auel – now at the IHS in Vienna, Angela Tacea and Anja Thomas) and our current and former colleagues at Maastricht University (especially Alexander Strelkov and Mathias Dobbels).

Special gratitude is due to the many administrators and politicians who made time for interviews or provided detailed written information.

Last, but not least, we would like to thank Maastricht University for its administrative support during our project, and the publishing team at Palgrave Macmillan for their patience and advice.

Abbreviations

ACTA	Anti-Counterfeiting Trade Agreement
CALRE	Conference of Legislative Assemblies of Regions
CDA	Christen Democratisch Appèl (Dutch Party)
CFSP	Common Foreign and Security Policy
COREPER	Committee of Permanent Representatives
COSAC	Conference of Parliamentary Committees for Union Affairs of Parliaments of the European Union
CSDP	Common Security and Defence Policy
D66	Democraten 66 (Dutch Party)
DG	Directorate-General
EAC	European Affairs Committee
ECJ	European Court of Justice
EMU	Economic and Monetary Union
EP	European Parliament
EU	European Union
EWS	Early Warning System
FTA	EU-Korea Free Trade Agreement
GFCM	General Fisheries Commission for the Mediterranean
IPEX	Platform for EU Inter-Parliamentary Exchange
JURI	EP Committee for Legal Affairs
MEP	Member of the European Parliament
MFF	Multiannual Financial Framework
MP	Member of Parliament
NPR	National Parliamentary Representative
OLP	Ordinary Legislative Procedure
OPAL	Observatory of Parliaments after the Lisbon Treaty
REGPEX	Information Exchange Platform of Regional Governments and Parliaments
RoP	Rules of Procedure
S&D	Socialists and Democrats
SMN	Subsidiarity Monitoring Network
STOA	Science and Technology Options Assessment (European Parliament)
TAB	Büro für Technikfolgen Abschätzung (Bundestag)

TEU	Treaty on European Union
TFEU	Treaty on the Functioning of the European Union
TFTP	Terrorist Finance Tracking Program
UK	United Kingdom
USA	United States of America

This page intentionally left blank

Introduction

Parliamentary administrations and the challenge of European integration: Introduction

Parliaments are an essential – indeed, a defining – element of democracy in Europe. In the political systems of most European states, democracy is, on the whole, understood as parliamentary democracy: legislatures elect executives and hold these to account, adopt legislation and approve budgets. Each national system operates differently; a number of semi-presidential systems provide exceptions, but, generally, the functioning of liberal democracy in Europe is based on the central role occupied by parliaments in most countries.

Beyond politics at the national level, within the institutional structure of the European Union (EU), the increasing powers of the European Parliament (EP) have been a key aspect of the wider integration process. As the EU evolved from an international organization into a novel polity, the empowerment of the EP has been the main plank in addressing the Union's putative 'democratic deficit'. The number of areas in which decisions are made jointly, through co-decision by national governments in the Council of the European Union and elected members in the EP, has been steadily expanding; since the Lisbon Treaty, this co-decision has, indeed, become the norm through the Ordinary Legislative Procedure. Beyond its legislative role, the EP has become a key actor in the EU through its powers in the appointment of the executive, in the adoption of annual budgets and multi-annual financial frameworks, and in approving international agreements – all developments which have contributed to the parliamentarization of the EU.

However, the process of democratizing the EU has not relied solely on delegating greater powers for the directly elected EP. Notwithstanding the advances made at the EU level, the challenge of legitimizing supranational governance in the EU is increasingly being seen as also requiring the involvement of national parliaments. In view of the distance between 'Brussels' and the citizens, the involvement of national parliaments in EU decision-making processes has increasingly come to be seen as a crucial remedy to legitimize further integration. The so-called Early Warning System (EWS), established by the Lisbon Treaty, formally recognized national parliaments as participants in EU affairs and provided them with non-binding rights to review and object to EU draft legislation (discussed in the next section). Even regional parliaments have become involved in the scrutiny of EU affairs, albeit in a more limited and selective manner.

In response to these developments, observers have noted the emergence of a multilevel parliamentary system (or field) in the EU – the presence and interaction between parliamentary bodies on different territorial levels in Europe (Crum and Fossum 2009; Winzen et al. 2012). Both in the political debate and in academic research, the 2010s have seen an upsurge regarding the role of parliaments in the EU, across a range of policy areas, and from a variety of normative and theoretical perspectives. In the context of a general trend towards greater Euroscepticism and public disenchantment with the EU (de Wilde and Trenz 2012), parliaments have become more active and more involved in EU processes, and there have been frequent calls for a greater role to be assigned at the national level (Groen and Christiansen 2015).

Such demand for further parliamentarization of the EU has come from various – even opposing – quarters. Eurosceptics see national parliaments as potential veto-players that may stop the further transfer of powers to the European level, or that may even help in 'repatriating' competences that have been granted to the EU. Others consider national parliaments essential in the further development of European integration by legitimizing the expanded role that intergovernmental bodies have accumulated, not least in the context of the response to the sovereign debt crisis in the Eurozone since 2010 (Auel and Christiansen 2015).

This recognition of the importance of parliaments in the EU, and the expectation that they may play an even greater role in the future, is remarkable against the background of a dominant discourse about the decline of parliaments. In the post-war era, a number of interrelated developments impacted on the traditional institutional setting within nation-states in a way that strengthened the role of the executive and marginalized legislatures (Moravcsik 1995; but see Judge 1995).

These developments include processes of globalization, the resultant growth of international interdependence of policy-making, the increasingly technical or scientific nature of governmental activity and the rise of the 'regulatory state', which has reduced the scope of majoritarian decision-making (Auel 2013: 3).

In Europe, these developments have occurred in the context of the wider process of European integration. In this perspective, the European integration process can be seen as an extreme version of international cooperation that has transferred decision-making from the domestic constitutional framework to the realm of the European level. This transfer from national to EU level has permitted executives – state leaders, ministers, diplomats and officials – to take decisions with less scrutiny than that to which they would be subject within the national domain. It is a process that has initially strengthened national executives and thus weakened national legislatures, with observers going as far as considering national parliaments as the 'losers' of the integration process (Maurer and Wessels 2001).

The challenge of European integration

Whereas in the earlier stages of European integration the constitutional position of national parliaments had been diminishing, the Lisbon Treaty marked a significant change, as it expanded institutional provisions in a number of ways. First, the Treaty included a 'Protocol on the Role of National Parliaments in the European Union' which mainly provides national parliaments with better access to information about the European decision-making process. Since then, national parliaments not only receive a broad range of documents, including non-legislative documents such as the annual reports of the Court of Auditors or the European Commission's annual legislative programme, but they also receive these documents directly (rather than via their governments).

Second, the 'Protocol on the Application of the Principles of Subsidiarity and Proportionality' provides national parliaments (both chambers in bicameral systems) with a more direct role in the EU legislative process through the EWS. They have the right to submit – within eight weeks of receiving a legislative proposal – a 'reasoned opinion' to the Commission if they find the proposal to violate the subsidiarity principle (Article 7.1). If one third of the national parliaments submit a reasoned opinion, the Commission must formally review the proposal and may withdraw or amend it, but it can also maintain it unaltered (Article 7.2). Thus, in these cases, national parliaments can only show the Commission the 'yellow card'; they cannot force the Commission to take their concerns into account. If, however, at least half of the national parliaments submit reasoned opinions on a legislative proposal falling under the ordinary legislative procedure (co-decision), and the Commission maintains the proposal, the legislative proposal will be submitted to both the Council and the EP for review (the 'orange card'). While national parliaments thus still do not have a right to force the Commission directly to take their opinion into account, this last rule enables parliaments to force the Council and the EP to deal with their concerns.

Regional parliaments are now also involved in EU policy-making for the first time: national parliaments are asked to consult regional parliaments with legislative powers before submitting their reasoned opinions under the EWS.

Third, according to Article 8 of the Protocol on the Application of the Principles of Subsidiarity and Proportionality, the European Court of Justice (ECJ) will have jurisdiction in actions on grounds of infringement of the principle of subsidiarity by a legislative act; such action can now also be brought forward by national parliaments through their governments.

Finally, national parliaments also obtained the right to veto the application of the passerelle clause (Article 48 para. 7), which covers the transition from unanimity to qualified majority or the transition from special to ordinary legislative procedure. National parliaments have to be informed at least six months before any decision is adopted and can (in this case, individually) veto the proposal within this time period (Auel and Christiansen 2015).

These new powers obtained by national and regional parliaments with the Lisbon Treaty, albeit essentially of a consultative nature, are a remarkable development, especially if viewed against the experience of decline since the beginning of European integration. As such, the Lisbon reforms can be regarded as a way of 'catching up' with national executives – and with an EP – that had previously made significant strides at the expense of national and regional parliaments. It is a process that has given national and regional parliaments more influence, though analysis has shown that not all of the promise of formal powers has actually been translated into tangible results in practice (Buzogány and Stuchlík 2011; Cooper 2012).

The advent of a greater European role has been a success for parliaments in the member states, but it also constitutes a major challenge for national and regional parliaments – institutions that had long been somewhat insulated from the integration process. In response to their new powers and the greater expectations of a presence in the context of EU politics, legislatures had to reform their internal procedures and invest in their resources. Responsibility to address EU matters had to expand from the 'ghetto' of specifically set-up European Affairs Committees to the parliament as a whole, meaning that other sectoral committees – and, indeed, the plenary as a whole – have increasingly had to concern themselves with EU-related decisions, something observers have identified as the mainstreaming of EU affairs (Gattermann et al. 2013).

The post-Lisbon process of the Europeanization of national and regional parliaments is ongoing, involving a continuous balancing act between the executive and legislative branches, and between the European, the national and the regional level (Goetz and Meyer-Sahling 2008). It involves a significant degree of inter-institutional cooperation, both horizontally (between national and regional parliaments and European institutions) and vertically (among national and regional parliaments across all member states). But there have also been signs of rivalry between institutions; for example, between the EP and the national parliaments, such as the question of how the role of the executive in the economic governance of the Eurozone should be scrutinized. This process is not finished and, hence, there are no permanent winners or losers but, rather, shifting sands of periodic advances and latent challenges affecting all players involved in this 'game' (Deubner 2013).

What is clear, however, is that the expectations – and pressures – on parliaments have greatly changed in the context of European integration. The tasks of national and regional parliaments have become significantly more demanding as the European integration process has advanced. These difficulties can be summarized in terms of three challenges to which parliaments have had to respond:

Accountability of national executives: Executives meet in opaque committee structures at the European level, and take decisions through qualified majority voting, making it ever more difficult for national parliaments to hold them to account (Auel et al. 2012).

Oversight of EU decision-making: The complex and occasionally byzantine decision processes at the EU level are very difficult to follow from the vantage point of national and regional parliaments which, until recently, did not have an independent presence in Brussels (Auel 2007).

Inter-parliamentary cooperation: The effective monitoring of EU affairs increasingly requires not only a horizontal line of communication – between national capitals and the EU institutions, but also a vertical one – among national parliaments from across the EU, in order to exchange information, compare assessments and coordinate strategies (Gattermann and Hefftler 2015). The same is, of course, true for regional parliaments.

Each of these three challenges has been difficult to address for national and regional parliaments. They require a recalibration of focus and energy among the elected members of parliament (MPs), new calculations of costs and benefits for political groups and individual members, and potentially difficult choices in terms of the engagement with, and criticism of, the process of integration. They also confront parliaments in the context of a phase of rising Euroscepticism and greater success for political parties and movements either openly critical of further integration, or hostile to EU membership of individual member states. In other words, parliaments are having to address the challenges of engaging more with Europe at a time when it is increasingly popular to disengage from Europe.

The European challenge for national and regional parliaments not only involves such political considerations, but also raises questions about party-political alignments, intra-party tensions and the political preferences of MPs. The challenge also raises the question of the capacity of parliaments as institutions to deal with the complexities and interdependencies of EU affairs. For national and regional parliaments to engage effectively with the EU requires not only political will, but also expertise, resources and funding. In other words, the European challenge for parliaments is not simply political, it is also administrative – it points the spotlight on an essential – but often overlooked – feature of national and regional parliaments: their administrations.

Parliaments are, of course, primarily political bodies and there is no doubt that the political dimension of their work – the activity of individual MPs, of political groups, of committees, of party leadership and of back benchers – is the dominant focus in the eyes of the public and the media, as well as in the analysis of academic scholars. It has, however, become unthinkable for parliaments to function effectively without considerable administrative support, and in the EU the challenges regarding accountability, oversight and cooperation make such support even more crucial. Arguably, in the EU's multilevel parliamentary field, national and regional parliaments have to have administrative resources in order to enable them to be politically influential players (Högenauer and Neuhold 2015).

It is perhaps something of a paradox that, in the post-Lisbon EU, the quality of democracy depends to some extent on the capacity of administrations – namely, the administrations of parliaments (Christiansen et al. 2014). This creates an intriguing conundrum, raising a number of interesting questions: 'How dependent are MPs on the support from administrators and clerks?' 'Are administrators in national and regional parliaments able to influence the scrutiny or decision-making processes?' 'Does their involvement encroach on the political authority of elected MPs?' 'Does the empowerment of bureaucratic actors within parliaments raise new questions about the democratic nature of EU decision-making?'

Objective of this book

The aim of this volume is to address these questions and, in the process, to illuminate the largely under-researched area of parliamentary administrations in Europe. We believe that shedding a light on the roles played by parliamentary administrators, and on the influence they exert, will make an important contribution to our understanding of the EU. Indeed, it fills a significant gap in the knowledge about the workings of multilevel democracy in Europe and we therefore also see this volume as a contribution to the evolving debate about the democratic legitimacy of European integration itself.

Our research straddles two long-standing but rather distinct strands in the academic literature: the work on legislatures, on the one hand, and research on bureaucracies, on the other. Until now, these strands have developed largely in isolation of one another: studies of parliaments and legislatures have traditionally had a strong – and, in the European context, almost exclusive – focus on the political dimension of their work. Research on bureaucracies, by contrast, has naturally tended to look at the executive branch: i.e. ministries, agencies and state administration more generally. In other words, scholars of parliamentary affairs have had little interest in administrations, and researchers working on bureaucracies have hardly ever looked at parliaments.

A focus on the role played by administrations of parliaments has therefore been largely absent from the radar of academic research. However, in the context of the challenges that parliaments in the EU face, such a focus is overdue and, indeed, urgent. This book seeks to close this gap, presenting new conceptual insights and original research in order to provide a first, comprehensive picture of parliamentary administrations in Europe.

In order to address the questions raised above, in Chapter 1 of this book we develop a conceptual framework that identifies a number of different roles that parliamentary administrators could possibly take on. These are derived from the academic literature of bureaucracies and have been adapted to the particular environment of national legislatures in the EU. Then, on the basis of this Introduction, we present the findings of the empirical research into a range of aspects of parliamentary administrations at all levels of the European parliamentary field. Separate chapters examine the role of administrators in the EP, in national parliaments and in regional assemblies. This includes the internal workings of EU affairs, and scrutiny within national and regional parliaments, as well as the networking of parliamentary administrators across Europe and in Brussels.

This research has been conducted in the context of collaborative fieldwork and has made use of a number of different research strategies and methodologies. First, we have conducted a survey of officials working in the administrations of national parliaments of all the member states, with a separate survey directed specifically at the staff working for assemblies in legislative regions. Second, we interviewed a large number of officials at the national and the European level. This included both the national parliamentary representatives in Brussels, as well as officials in a number of member states. With regard to the latter, officials in nine member states in particular (Germany, the Netherlands, Belgium, Denmark, the UK, France, Italy, Poland and Slovakia) were interviewed on their experiences with EU affairs. Finally, our research also benefited from the in-depth document research that was conducted in the context of the OPAL project on all 28 member states (see www.opal-europe.org/ for details). These various channels have provided us with a rich foundation of original empirical material, which, together with a comprehensive reading of the secondary literature relevant to the various aspects of our study, allows us to make authoritative statements about the role of parliamentary administrations in European integration.

However, before presenting the findings of our original research, it is worthwhile presenting a brief review of the existing literature in the areas of parliamentarism and bureaucracies. As argued earlier, these two fields of research have developed along somewhat distinct trajectories but, in order to make the link between these, we believe it is valuable to explore existing avenues and openings that might already be present. In the following section, we therefore take a closer look at the state of play with respect to these two literatures, as a way of preparing the ground for the kind of linkages we seek to develop subsequently.

The study of parliamentary affairs in the European Union

As indicated, in the context of addressing the EU's 'democratic deficit' and thereby bringing Europe closer to the citizens, the role of national parliaments in EU decision-making has been upgraded in recent years. National parliaments have acquired new powers to review and object to draft legislative acts, building on earlier provisions introduced by the Maastricht and Amsterdam treaties, as well as on the Barroso initiative that followed the failed ratification of the Constitutional Treaty (Kaczynski 2011). Indeed, the experience of the constitutional convention that prepared the draft Constitutional Treaty was a watershed for parliamentarians in the EU, given that they featured prominently among its membership. Even though the Constitutional Treaty did not come to pass, the largely unchanged Lisbon Treaty eventually brought additional powers for national parliaments into the EU system.

The gradual expansion of the powers of national parliaments has been reflected in the scholarly debate. Following accounts of how parliaments were the 'victims' of European integration due to a process of 'de-parliamentarization' (Moravcsik 1995; Weber-Panariello 1995; Norton 1996) in the 1990s, national parliaments have been portrayed as more active players in the context of EU integration following the Treaty of Amsterdam (e.g. Auel and Benz 2005; O'Brennan and Raunio 2007), although some still raise the question as to whether national parliaments are 'losers or late-comers' (Maurer and Wessels 2001) or, indeed, whether they are 'destined for irrelevance' (Raunio 2010).

In this context, attempts have also been made to classify national parliaments according to their formal legal powers and to explain variation across the EU with regard to the way in which the executive can be held to account (Maurer and Wessels 2001; Kiiver 2006). The introduction of the 'Open Method of Coordination' (Benz 2007; de Ruiter 2010) and more recent reforms through treaty change have opened up new areas of research (e.g. Cooper 2006, 2012; Raunio 2007; Rothenberger and Vogt 2007; Kiiver 2011, 2012). This has also involved a greater degree of specialization, with publications focused on specific aspects such as the role of upper chambers in EU scrutiny (de Ruiter 2014), the involvement of regional assemblies (Vara Arribas and Högenauer 2015), or new developments in EU affairs inter-parliamentary cooperation (Hefftler and Gattermann 2015).

Since Lisbon, much attention has obviously focused on the functioning and effectiveness of the EWS. This initially involved contributions from both political science and law that were concerned with the formal arrangements and the implementation of the system as the Lisbon Treaty came into force (Raunio 2011; Kiiver 2012). Once the system started to operate, and it became clear that the number of 'yellow cards' would not be all that great, scholars responded with sceptical assessments of the impact that the system could have (de Wilde 2012). The focus here was on the limited political benefit that MPs could expect from their involvement in these procedures, as well as on the uneven uptake of the new powers among parliaments in the EU. Much of the activity in the context of the EWS was concentrated among just one third of the national chambers in the EU, making it rare for reasoned opinions to reach the threshold of votes required by the treaty.

In addition, as scholars have pointed out, the EWS is limited to the scrutiny of the application of the subsidiarity principle, not the substantive content of draft legislation. Furthermore, 'yellow cards' are not binding on the European Commission; in fact, the Commission has on occasion made the point that the real power to block legislative proposals from the Commission lies with the Council. Given that in most member states parliamentary majorities are reflected in government positions, this arrangement further reduces the incentives for MPs to devote limited time and political capital to the EWS. The flipside of this coin is, however, that the EWS does provide opposition parties in national parliaments with a new source of influence – be it through improved access to information or through additional opportunities for external representation.

Once the EWS had been in place for some years, and as more information has become available on its operation, the focus of research has moved on from the emphasis on formal powers to the study of the actual practice (Auel and Christiansen 2015). Empirical research has focused on gathering data about the context within which individual chambers have adopted reasoned opinions, in order to link this to the incidence of possible explanatory factors such as the level of Euroscepticism or the formal powers of parliaments within the respective domestic constitutional framework (Gattermann and Hefftler 2015). In addition, there has also been a renewed interest in the way in which national parliaments hold national officials to account, as these become involved in the decision-making structure of the Council of Ministers. The incidence and effects of parliamentary scrutiny reserves in the proceedings of Council working groups and of the Committee of Permanent Representatives (COREPER) have been used as a measure of this involvement.

Another avenue for research has been placing the focus on the 'reverse effect' of the EWS – to direct study not on what national parliaments may or may not be able to achieve in Europe but, rather, the way in which Europe has impacted on the workings of national parliaments (Auel and Benz 2005; Goetz and Meyer-Sahling 2008). Such a focus is behind the observed trend towards the mainstreaming of EU affairs, the changing roles of parliamentary committees and political parties in the process of EU scrutiny, and the creation of new channels for inter-parliamentary cooperation. This line of scholarly investigation has put earlier scepticism towards the EWS into perspective: whereas national parliaments continue to have limited direct influence on EU decision-making, the introduction of the EWS has had a noticeable impact on the way in which national parliaments work internally, and how they cooperate with one another (Christiansen et al. 2014).

With respect to horizontal cooperation among parliaments, scholars have brought new empirical insights to the long-standing study of the Conference of Parliamentary Committees for Union Affairs of Parliaments of the European Union (COSAC), the Speakers' Conference and the pan-European families of political parties – instances of inter-parliamentary cooperation that preceded the creation of the EWS but that have been reinvigorated by renewed activity. Recent research has also identified parliamentary officials as having a growing role in facilitating inter-parliamentary cooperation (Högenauer and Neuhold 2015). Almost all national parliaments now have permanent representatives based in the EP in Brussels, each on the whole working separately from their member state's EU embassy. Their close interaction constitutes the more visible part of a growing network of parliamentary officials across the EU, exchanging information, coordinating scrutiny strategies and, on occasion, even managing a 'division of labour' with regard to the EU's legislative agenda.

At the same time, while the EWS may have triggered greater academic interest in the role of national parliaments in Europe, recent research has broadened the scope significantly beyond the narrow confines of legislative scrutiny. Scholars have looked at the frequency with which EU matters have been debated in the plenaries and the committees of national parliaments as a measure of the level of their involvement in the integration process (Auel et al. 2015). Research on parliamentary debates has also contributed to the study of discourses about European integration more generally (Wendler 2014).

In the same vein, scholars have gone beyond the study of legislative scrutiny to assess parliamentary activity in a range of non-legislative aspects of EU policy-making. A prominent area here has been the way in which national parliaments have developed an interest in European foreign policy. Numerous publications have addressed various aspects of this question, demonstrating both the rising interest and the limited effectiveness that parliamentary involvement has in this area (Bono 2005; Peters et al. 2010; Huff 2015). This also includes the attention that has been bestowed on the Inter-Parliamentary Conference on Common Foreign and Security Policy (CFSP), which brings together national MPs and European MEPs in debating key issues on the policy agenda (Herranz Surralés 2014; Stavridis 2014).

Even greater attention has been devoted to the evolving area of economic governance in the EU, specifically in the context of the sovereign debt crisis in the Eurozone. A new inter-parliamentary committee of MPs and MEPs was set up here as well, but more significant has been the research into the way in which, domestically, parliaments have been affected by the impact of the radical changes in the external environment (Crum 2013). The crisis has had discrete effects across the member states of the EU, not only in terms of the divide between Eurozone members and non-members, but also with regard to donor and programme countries within the Eurozone. Research has demonstrated that rather than having a universal impact on parliaments – for example, by constituting a further step in the process of de-parliamentarization – the effect has been uneven: while parliaments in some member states have been negatively affected, others have actually seen an increase in their powers in this context (Auel and Höing 2015). The German Bundestag is a prominent example of the latter case.

Research across a variety of more specialized aspects of parliamentary involvement in the EU has been matched by a number of broader and encompassing publications. While some of these have sought to develop new conceptual insights, the general aim has been to bring together a diverse range of scholarship and provide comprehensive overviews of the state of play in the field (Crum and Fossum 2013; Cygan 2013). Most notable in this regard is the *Palgrave Handbook of National Parliaments and the European Union* which, in addition to a number of chapters on cross-cutting issues, comprises individual chapters on all 28 member states, providing detailed accounts of how parliaments deal with EU affairs in each case (Hefftler et al. 2015).

In sum, there has been a remarkable growth in the body of literature on parliamentary affairs in Europe: from the marginal attention that parliaments received only a few years ago, this literature has grown enormously, arguably out of proportion to the actual influence that parliaments have in EU decisions and the attention they give to European affairs themselves. It is a clear recognition that, for scholars, the democratic dimension of European integration continues to matter, and future reforms may well be required in order to address questions about the legitimacy of intergovernmental decision-making and technocratic governance in the EU. Attention to the administrative dimension has been very limited though, and, so far, there has not been any systematic treatment of parliamentary administrations in the EU.

The study of public administration in the European Union

While this book seeks to add to our understanding of the role of parliaments in the EU, it also contributes to the growing body of literature on public administration in the EU – a literature that has developed significantly since the late 1990s. From an almost exclusive focus on the European Commission, it has expanded into several other areas of the EU's institutional architecture, while also producing increasingly sophisticated studies of the Commission itself (Hooghe 2001; Kassim et al. 2013). From general treatments of the Commission as an actor in the integration process, there has been a move to study the organization, with specific focus on particular aspects such as the role of the president (and the observed trend towards presidentialization) (Ross 1995; Peterson 2011), the bureaucratic politics pitching different parts of the administration against one another (Christiansen 1997), the influence of seconded staff (Trondal et al. 2008), the presence of party politics among the Commissioners in the College (Bauer and Ege 2012) and the evolution of ethical standards in the Commission's administration (Cini 1996). The value of these contributions has been to demonstrate that the Commission is not the unitary actor which it is often assumed to be, but that it is subject to numerous internal divisions and also to changes over time. With respect to the latter, there have also been interesting observations about the potential for Euroscepticism and the lack of initiative – challenging prior assumptions in integration theory about the presumed 'institutional self-interest' of the Commission to expand its powers (Dehousse and Thompson 2012).

Another trend has been to look at the relationship between the Commission and other actors from an administrative science perspective. This has included studies of the Commission's relations not only to other EU institutions (Christiansen 2001), but also to organized interests (Coen and Richardson 2009), external experts (Gornitzka and Sverdrup 2008), representatives from third countries (Dimier and McGeever 2006) and the media (Bijsmans and Altides 2007). In this context, the evolution of the Commission has been seen in the context of studying the independence, transparency, accountability or efficiency of the supranational administration (Wille 2010).

The relationship between the European Commission and the national administrations deserves a special mention here, as it has been the source not only of empirical research, but also of theoretical development. The close cooperation between civil servants from the national and the European level, specifically in the context of hundreds of implementing committees working out the details of legislative implementation, has been regarded as evidence of an 'administrative fusion' between these two levels (Wessels 1998; Christiansen 2011). A related aspect has been the study of the Europeanization of national administrations, as these come to grips with the impact that European integration has had within the member states (Börzel and Risse 2000; Graziano and Vink 2008).

However, beyond the focus on the Commission, there has been growing interest in the wider administrative domain of the EU, with a number of publications addressing the EU administration, or, as some scholars have termed it, the 'executive order' as a whole (Curtin and Egeberg 2008). The aim here has been to identify political, organizational or sociological patterns that might apply to the whole of the EU's administration, in juxtaposition to individual institutions and also to national administrations. Another focus has been on the impact that the accession of new member states has had on the institutions of the Union (Best et al. 2008), something that has become more relevant as the capacity of the EU to accommodate new members started to affect the debate about enlargement from the 1990s onwards.

At the same time, there has also been greater attention to detailed studies of other institutions. First among these is the focus on EU agencies, both single-case and comparative studies of specific agencies, and analysis of the wider phenomenon of 'agencification' in the EU (Groenleer 2009; Busuioc et al. 2011; Rittberger and Wonka 2013). The various 'waves' of agency creation in the EU, going hand in hand with the expansion of competences (but also with the more limited role of the European Commission under Barroso), has attracted significant scholarly interest, including also comparisons with developments in the member states and in the USA (Shapiro 1997). Furthermore, scholars have looked at the evolving role of the General Secretariat of the Council (Christiansen and Vanhoonacker 2008) and, more recently, at the creation and early years of the European External Action Service (Duke 2009, 2012), with some studies also looking at the European Central Bank (Hodson 2015), the Ombudsman's Office (Curtin 2007) and the administration of the ECJ (Naômé 2008).

This brief review of the literature demonstrates that there has been a significant deepening and widening of the research on the EU's administrative system over recent decades. However, compared with the significant body of literature that has accumulated on public administration in the EU, rather little attention has been devoted to the administration of the European Parliament – with a few notable exceptions (Dobbels and Neuhold 2013; Egeberg et al. 2013), and even less on the role of the administrations of national parliaments involved in the European integration process (but see Högenauer and Christiansen 2015). Scholars have presented their research on the nature and identity of the parliamentary staff, and on the administrative resources that parliaments devote to the scrutiny of the European executive.

This still leaves the need for the kind of comprehensive analysis of the role that parliamentary administrations play in the context of the EU's system of multilevel governance, and which this books seeks to provide. This review of the literature also confirms the earlier point about the gap between studies of parliamentary affairs and studies of public administration, specifically in the context of European integration. We have rich knowledge of the role of European and national parliaments and of the EU's administrative system, but hardly any connection between these two bodies of literature. It is in this regard that the present volume seeks to build a bridge through the systematic and comprehensive study of parliamentary administrations at the regional, national and European levels.

Conclusion

This volume seeks to build on the formidable scholarship that has been devoted to the study of parliaments and administrations in the EU, bringing these together in a focus on parliamentary administration. In Chapter 1, we develop an analytical framework for the study of parliamentary administration that is derived from models of different roles that administrators may carry out – models which were designed for the study of national executives, but which are being adapted here for a systematic analysis of the roles of parliamentary officials.

Chapter 1 applies this model to the EP, making use of a number of case studies that demonstrate the way in which the staff of the EP has been involved in the internal decision-making surrounding the legislative process inside the parliament. Chapters 2, 3 and 4 are devoted to the activities of the administrators of national parliaments and their evolving roles in the context of EU integration. Chapter 3 focuses on the administrative dimension of inter-parliamentary cooperation, charting the rising number and relevance of national parliamentary representatives in Brussels. Chapter 4 looks more directly at the administrations of national parliaments in a comparative perspective, bringing together both qualitative material from the various domestic arenas and original statistical data on the size and resources of parliamentary administrations. The aim here is to make statements about the convergence or divergence in the roles of parliamentary administrators across the EU. Chapter 5 takes this analysis one step further by applying the model developed in Chapter 1 to parliamentary administrations and identifying each member state in terms of the analytical categories of different roles. This analysis is further strengthened by in-depth examination of a number of specific chambers: the German Bundestag, the Danish Folketing, the Dutch Tweede Kamer and the Austrian parliament.

Chapter 6 finally brings the analysis one level further down, by looking at regional assemblies and the roles of their administrations in the EU context. While this is also an encompassing chapter, the focus is necessarily on the eight member states with regions that have legislative powers, and hence a greater propensity to be affected by, and involved in, EU decision-making. The chapter provides original material, both statistical data and interview-based research, in order to offer a comprehensive account of the way in which the administrators of regional assemblies support the EU involvement of their regions. The picture here is mixed: while regions with legislative powers have, as do national parliaments, also become more active players in EU affairs, the secretariats of their assemblies tend to struggle with limited resources and the often low salience that EU matters have for their members.

The Conclusion to the book brings together the findings from all three levels of analysis and, based on the insights derived from this research, provides some overall conclusions concerning the role of parliamentary administrators in the EU.

1
Conceptualizing the Role of Parliamentary Administrators

Introduction

The Treaty of Lisbon acknowledged the role of national parliaments in the democratic functioning of the EU and strengthened their formal involvement in EU policy-making, most notably through better information rights and the creation of the EWS. These new opportunities led to greater academic attention and contributed to a growing literature on the role of national parliaments in the EU (e.g. Hefftler et al. 2015) and the contribution that these could make in helping to address the EU's putative 'democratic deficit' (Bellamy and Kröger 2013).

The existing literature on European parliaments has largely focused on their political functions (e.g. Auel and Raunio 2014), on the roles of different political actors within parliaments and on the impact of party politics on parliaments (Hix 1999; Raunio 2002; Holzhacker 2005; Hix and Høyland 2013; Bellamy and Kröger 2014). However, just like state executives, parliaments are not *purely* political creatures. After all, it is widely acknowledged that bureaucracy is an essential part of modern states and societies (Arnold 1987), and with the rise of the bureaucratic state has come the growth of parliamentary administrations. These may be of a much smaller size than governmental bureaucracies and their activity may be less visible, but parliaments – like governments – do have bureaucracies of their own. This observation raises a number of questions that have not been answered conclusively in the existing literature: What role do these officials play within the legislatures in which they work, and how can we conceptualize the nature of this particular aspect of parliaments?

The aim of this chapter is to review the key literature on the roles of parliamentary officials, in order to develop a conceptual framework that allows us to capture the tasks of parliamentary officials in EU affairs.

The key question that guides this effort is, in particular, how technical or political the tasks of administrators are – that is, how much influence they can potentially have on the scrutiny of EU affairs. For this purpose, the existing literatures on administrative roles in executive and parliamentary administrations will be reviewed. On this basis, more refined typologies of the tasks of officials in the EP and national parliaments are then developed.

The problem of delegation to administrators

Studies on bureaucracy often refer to the type of bureaucracy as idealized in the work of Max Weber. The Weberian ideal of a bureaucracy is characterized by hierarchical structures and the rule of law. The personnel of this type of bureaucracy are career officials recruited by way of 'objective criteria and educational qualifications' (Barberis 2011: 15). These professionals adhere to principles of neutrality (Weber 1978, in Barberis 2011). However, this idea of a neutral civil service has been questioned and there is an extensive debate about the need for, and the ways of, controlling policy decisions that are delegated by elected politicians to the bureaucracy (Boehmke et al. 2005: 149).

The literature on the delegation of powers to bureaucrats postulates that the complexity of the modern state and the issues at stake in policy-making require politicians to delegate certain tasks and decisions due to a lack of time and expertise. As a corollary of such delegation, governments often face a tension between the need to maintain political control and the value of bureaucratic expertise (Huber and McCarty 2004).

At the heart of this debate is the so-called 'principal-agent problem', which originates conceptually from economic analysis and concerns ways of minimizing risks in the presence of moral hazard (Grossman and Hart 1983). As Kassim and Menon (2003) point out, the principal-agent model has become the dominant model to probe into the challenges arising from contracting or risk-sharing (Grossman and Hart 1983) in any setting or context. Agency relationships are established when one actor or a set of actors (the principal) delegates a set of tasks to a second party (the agent), based on a contractual agreement (Kassim and Menon 2003: 122). Prime examples in this context are delegation of powers to executive agencies or the delegation within the executive, where policies are in practice often drawn up and managed by the civil service rather than by elected politicians.

A similar challenge confronts elected representatives in legislatures, who also need to delegate certain decisions due to time constraints

(Arnold 1987: 279). Delegation to staff within parliaments is also necessitated by the fact that the limited number of MPs are at a disadvantage compared with the much larger ministries that they are supposed to control.

The principal-agent model has been applied to the US Congress, with its elected members seen as the principal and the bureaucracy seen as the agent (e.g. McCubbins and Page 1987; Moe 1984, 1987). Here, principals are faced with the possibility of the administration developing policies deviating from the original mandate, a trend that has been coined as 'bureaucratic drift'. Such drift is a principal-agent problem that questions the extent to which political actors are able to ensure that their original intentions will indeed be carried out by the administrative staff (McCubbins et al. 1987).

In this context, the concept of 'optimal delegation' to bureaucrats is of relevance. Boehmke et al., when developing a model of policy-making, recognized multiple sources of information – from the bureaucracy, an interest group – and their respective impact on policy-making (Boehmke et al. 2005: 140). This helped them to address the legislature's optimal delegation problem: 'legislative preferences over agency policy choices'. In particular, they observe that the legislature has a slight preference for an agency with preferences closer to those of the legislature than one that differs from those of the legislature (Boehmke et al. 2005: 141). They also raise the point that legislative delegation can be desirable. This is so because the agency to whom authority is 'delegated may be more expert than the legislature itself'. Agencies moreover tend to integrate various input by lobbyists and this can 'lead to better informed choices when policy-making' (Boehmke et al. 2005: 162).

For political actors, the main risk that poses itself is such that 'the very skills and expertise that bureaucrats enjoy create the possibility that bureaucrats will usurp the rightful role of politicians in policy-making processes' (Huber and McCarty 2004). An excessive amount of bureaucratic influence can ultimately challenge democratic principles, which is why the literature has devoted much attention to questions of political control and oversight. The literature on the US Congress in particular has produced valuable concepts and insights, albeit in the context of the control of parliament over executive bureaucrats in agencies – that is, bureaucrats that are external to the functioning of the parliament itself. In this regard, three approaches in particular stand out:

- First, Arnold introduced a distinction between statutory oversight techniques, non-statutory techniques, and administrative rules and procedures. Statutory techniques involve the use of authorization or re-authorization bills or budgetary bills to provide guidelines or to place prohibitions on agencies. Non-statutory techniques comprise the use of hearings and reports to control bureaucratic activity. Finally, administrative rules and procedures allow legislatures to make agencies transparent and create channels of appeal for interested parties (Arnold 1987: 208–10).

- Second, McCubbins and Schwartz distinguish between 'police patrol' and 'fire alarm' oversight. Police patrol oversight requires the legislature regularly to check samples of an agency's work, whereas fire alarm oversight relies on citizens and interested parties examining administrative decisions. A system of rules and procedures allows access to information and establishes rights of appeal (McCubbins and Schwartz 1984: 166).
- Finally, in the context of governments and executives, Huber distinguishes between ex ante and ex post institutions. Ex ante institutions kick in before civil servants take action, whereas ex post institutions serve as a remedy. One ex ante remedy would be to allow politicians to select suitable (and potentially politicized) civil servants who sympathize with the views of the politician or government. Other ex-ante measures involve administrative rules and tight legislation. Ex post instruments include hearings and courts. Budgetary powers can be used both to allow and to prevent certain actions by the agent (Huber 2000: 399–401).

Overall, the different classifications overlap and can be combined as presented in Table 1.1.

Table 1.1 Parliamentary oversight over executive bureaucracies

	Ex-ante (prevention)	**Ex-post (correction)**
Statutory	• Tight laws • Reauthorization bills • Budget	• Budget
Non-statutory	• Politicized appointments	• Hearings • Reports • Appeal to courts
Admin. rules and procedures	• On consultations and stakeholder hearings	• On transparency • On appeals

Note: Based on Arnold 1987, McCubbins and Schwartz 1984, Huber 2000; cf. Högenauer and Neuhold (2013), 'National Parliaments after Lisbon: Administrations on the Rise?', OPAL Online Paper 12/2013.

However, this literature on *executive* civil servants does not describe political oversight over *parliamentary* civil servants well. Most of the mechanisms are too formalistic to govern the relationship between politicians and staff within the same institution. In addition, political oversight in the case of agencies is about controlling administrators when they implement and manage policies after parliament has adopted a legislative decision. In the case of parliamentary staff, and in particular in the context of the scrutiny of European affairs, the challenge is to control administrative activity and input before parliamentary decisions. In the context of EU affairs, parliamentary staff is usually involved in the preparation of a parliamentary decision, rather than in the long-term management of policies. Thus, the use of laws, the re-authorization of bills and administrative rules on appeals, transparency and stakeholder hearings is applicable only in the context of policy-related activity where decision-making is delegated to bureaucrats.

The instruments available for political oversight over parliamentary administrations are therefore somewhat different. In order to avoid internal conflict, national parliaments generally try to ensure that parliamentary staff is politically neutral and at the service of all parties. The ex-ante measures can take the form of rules on the political neutrality of civil servants and politically neutral appointments.

One of the main forms of control and oversight available to politicians in parliaments is trust. As politicians take the final decisions in legislatures, it is in their power to follow administrative advice or to discard it. Accordingly, it is in the power of political actors not to accept advice provided by officials if it becomes apparent that the latter are politically biased. Administrators, in turn, will anticipate that their influence depends on the extent to which they are trusted and will try to avoid any blatant bias (DeGregorio 1994: 2; Winzen 2011). Trust is strongest where administrators adhere to a written or unwritten professional code that includes transparency and neutrality as its core principles. However, lack of trust is more likely to have negative consequences on the influence of administrators if bigger – and especially governing – parties mistrust them. Manley's study of politically biased committee staff in Congress illustrates that the opposition can do little to check staff as long as the staff is supported by the majority (1968).

In this context, Gailmard and Patty's research into the conditions under which delegation works best is useful. Based on a formal model, the authors show that the risks of delegation are held in check if issues are delegated to officials that have 'some measure of control over policy issues they care about'. Accordingly, politicized competence is the best 'kind available in equilibrium' (Gailmard and Patty 2007: 886). The model developed builds on the assumption that officials are motivated to varying degrees to invest in their career. They are thus either policy motivated 'zealots' or policy indifferent 'slackers' (Gailmard and Patty 2007: 874). Within a regime of 'politicized competence', zealots – and only zealots – invest in developing expertise and remain in the bureaucracy throughout their careers. A main incentive for zealots to invest in their expertise accordingly is a merit system that is based on job tenure protections combined with discretion-setting by the legislature (Gailmard and Patty 2007: 875). Note that politicized competence as conceived by Gailmard and Patty (2007) is not to be confused with politicization and partisanship but, rather, is to be seen as the willingness of officials to develop their policy expertise.

The fact that political oversight in parliaments thus relies predominantly on informal mechanisms highlights two other aspects about delegation: First, in order for a positive relationship between politicians and staff to develop, it is important that staff acts – at least to some extent – according to a logic of appropriateness, and accepts and internalizes principles of neutrality and transparency (Olsen 2006). Second, when studying these processes it is particularly important to know whether extensive delegation to administrators – beyond merely 'technical' tasks – takes place in the first place. Therefore, in this volume we seek to establish the types of task that are delegated to parliamentary administrators.

The literature on delegation suggests that delegation is particularly likely to occur in the context of complex issues and those of low salience (Manley 1968) – which implies a high level of delegation to parliamentary administrators in EU affairs, as these are perceived by parliaments as being both complex and of low (electoral) salience. In addition, a further incentive may lie in the desire of parliaments to reduce their dependence on the information provided by governments, something which even leads majority parties to be in favour of parliaments gathering information independent of governments (Interview 1). Finally, the Lisbon changes, and especially the EWS, require parliaments to handle an increased amount of information, to identify priorities and to react to proposed EU legislation within a narrow time span (eight weeks). As this scrutiny is limited to objections on the grounds of subsidiarity, the resultant reasoned opinions need to be based on legal justifications. Thus, if parliaments want to make use of these new opportunities effectively as a means of maximizing their influence within EU affairs, they may need to rely on administrators to carry out such tasks (cf. Christiansen et al. 2014).

However, the literature on national parliaments in Europe provides few insights into the roles that administrators might play. Parliamentary administrations in Western Europe have so far been the subject of mainly descriptive analysis (Campbell and Laporte 1981; Ryle 1981; Harfst and Schnapp 2003; Perez 2007). Baron (2013) highlights the emphasis on political neutrality in the French system, and mentions both an advisory role and an increasing involvement in the drafting of laws, amendments and reports. Independence and autonomy from governments are essential characteristics of not only the French, but also the British parliamentary administrative system (Campbell and Laporte 1981; Ryle 1981; Perez 2007). By contrast, in Germany, the civil service of parliament is covered by the same legal framework as the federal bureaucracy, which allows for mobility between the legislative and executive bureaucracy (Blischke 1981). For the administration of the US Congress, Patterson describes the tasks as information-gathering, the planning of hearings and drafting (Patterson 1970: 26)

Alternative resources in the literature are the typologies that have been developed with regard to bureaucrats in executives and the nascent literature on the EP. Page and Jenkins, for example, develop a typology of policy roles in the context of mid-level bureaucrats in the UK. Building on sociological theories of bureaucracy and drawing on 140 interviews, they have identified three types of policy role of middle-level administrators working for UK ministries (Page and Jenkins 2005: 60–71). These include:

- a *production role,* which consists mainly of drawing up policy drafts and documents;
- a *maintenance role,* which comprises trying to ensure that policies run according to agreed principles within ministerial bureaucracies; and
- a *service role,* which consists of offering knowledge, advice and skills to those involved in policy-making. Providing advice to the executive can be seen as the clearest manifestation of the service role (Page and Jenkins 2005: 71).

While the production and service roles are thus likely to be also relevant in a parliamentary context, the maintenance role seems to be a typical executive role.

Towards an analysis of the roles of officials in the European Parliament

The literature on the EP may also be instructive for studying the role of officials in national parliaments in EU affairs. Even though the EP is a transnational body, it is nevertheless a legislature that performs similar functions to those of national parliaments. Officials both in the EP and in national parliaments have to grapple with the technicalities and complexities of EU legislation and the decision-making process. According to Provan (2001, cited in Neunreither 2006: 55), assistance to EP Committees and MEPs can be broken down into technical-administrative assistance – which consists of organizational support, technical-substantive assistance – which involves procedural advice and assistance with drafting and research assistance and, lastly, political assistance – which is defined as political coordination within or across political groups and policy definition.

Provan recommended that political assistance be left to the staff of political groups and the assistants of MEPs (ibid.). This breakdown is detailed, but the description of all tasks that might fall to the parliamentary administration as 'technical' might downplay the role of the core EP administration and hide the extent to which decisions are delegated.

Winzen questions more openly the extent to which the work of the EP staff is merely technical or also of relevance to public policy and, in the process, defines two roles: managing the process and informing the process (Winzen 2011). This distinction between 'technical' and 'non-technical' is, however, rather basic – at least at first glance. Egeberg et al. (2013) also examine the activities of EP staff by way of an online survey (N = 118). When zooming in on what officials actually do – that is, what tasks they (claim to) perform – it becomes apparent that providing background information for MEPs ranks at the top, followed by the drafting of documents (Egeberg et al. 2013) (see also Chapter 2, for an overview of this debate).

Finally, Dobbels and Neuhold (2013; Neuhold and Dobbels 2014) have attempted to apply the roles developed by Page and Jenkins to the EP (see Table 1.2). For the EP, the production role would imply mainly the drawing up of meeting documents and drafts, whereas a service role would also involve supplying personal and specific knowledge to MEPs on the substance of the draft reports – for example, when it comes to questions related to a specific policy. Moreover, procedural guidance is also crucial in a parliament that co-legislates with the Council on matters covering more than 85 treaty articles. Finally, the

Table 1.2 Roles and tasks of officials of the EP secretariat under the ordinary legislative procedure

Roles	Production	Service	Steering
Tasks	• Preparation of draft reports and meeting documents • Compilation of amendments • Drawing up of voting lists • Making calculations (e.g. for the annual budget) • Preparation of trialogue meetings	• (Extensive) Briefing of MEPs on compromise proposals to be launched • Provision of in-depth advice on policy issues • (Extensive) Procedural guidance	• Tabling potential compromises to be proposed at certain stages of (inter-institutional) negotiations • Direct intervention in inter-institutional negotiations (e.g. with the Council)
Extent of involvement in policy-making	Low–medium	Medium–high	High

Note: *These observations and classifications are based on the case studies presented in Chapter 2.

authors suggest that EP officials could perform a steering role. This would imply that EP civil servants substantially influence policy beyond the instructions of MEPs (or because of the lack thereof) and possibly even intervene directly in negotiations with the Council (for more details, see Chapter 2).

Parliamentary administrations in national and regional parliaments

In the case of national and regional parliaments, the same shortcomings in the existing literature remain relevant. It seems that most of the existing typologies only partially fit the purpose of describing parliamentary staff. Either they are too descriptive and simply list various tasks in the absence of an explanation of how these matter, or the proposed categories are very broad and risk missing distinctions that could be relevant for the role of parliamentary staff involved in the scrutiny of EU affairs.

In order to capture the differences between parliamentary administrations in a meaningful way, we need to step back from overly broad and catch-all categories, such as 'technical' and 'non-technical'. This is important for a number of reasons: first, with such undifferentiated categories, there is a risk that all observations might fall into the same category. In that case, the categories are unhelpful, as they do not further our understanding of parliamentary administrations and their different set-ups. Second, we would not be able to capture nuances in the extent to which tasks of parliamentary administrations really are 'non-technical' and therefore border on the political. This is particularly important as those functions are potentially problematic from a delegation perspective: when administrators perform 'non-technical' functions, certain elements of parliamentary scrutiny are no longer performed by elected officials.

In addition, one of the specificities of national parliaments is that much of EU affairs scrutiny increasingly revolves around the provision of large amounts of information by EU institutions direct to national parliaments. Therefore, information-processing is becoming a key challenge for national parliaments and now forms a central part of the tasks of parliamentary administrations. However, information-processing can take various forms, having different implications for administrative input. As a result, we decided to follow a largely inductive approach to develop a refined typology of roles on the basis of both the existing literature and our own empirical insights into the tasks of administrators in the political process.

The issue of information-processing is even more central in the case of regional parliaments. In Protocol 2 of the Lisbon Treaty, national parliaments are asked to consult with their regional parliaments under the Lisbon Treaty where appropriate. Thus, whether regional parliaments are consulted or not depends essentially on the degree of decentralization within individual member states. At the time of writing, there are eight EU member states in which regional parliaments have legislative powers, and where regional parliaments are therefore involved in the EWS: Germany, Austria, Belgium, Italy, Spain, the United Kingdom, Finland and Portugal. In these cases, regional parliaments receive those EU legislative proposals that affect their competences. For these institutions, the amount of information coming from Brussels is an even greater challenge than for national parliaments, given their more limited resources (cf. Chapter 6).

Conceptualizing the roles and tasks of parliamentary administrations in Europe

We can distinguish between five ideal types of roles related to information-processing (cf. Table 1.3). These distinctions are based on

Table 1.3 Roles and tasks of parliamentary administrators in EU affairs

Roles	**Administrative Assistant**	**Analyst**	**Advisor**	**Agenda-shaper**	**Coordinator**
Tasks	• Gathers and forwards information • Summarizes information • Organizes committee meetings	• Provides choice of balanced arguments* • Drafts after debates* • Procedural and legal advice	• Content-related advice • Drafts before debates*	• Preselection of documents	• Coordination with executive • Internal coordination (e.g. within bi-cameral parliaments) • With other parliaments • With EU institutions
Extent of involvement in scrutiny	Low	Low–medium	Medium	Medium–high	

Note: *These tasks and distinctions were derived from the interview data.

an analysis of the Lisbon provisions and possible implications for administrations:

- First, under an administrative assistant model, the administration would either simply forward the information from the European level or government to the relevant committees and to MPs without further comment, or provide politicians with very short summaries as regards to content of the respective measure. In both cases, the opportunities for steering the discussion in a particular direction would be absent or limited. Parliamentary scrutiny is fully in the hands of elected MPs, which diminishes the risks of runaway bureaucracies. At the same time, elected MPs receive little support from the administration, which may limit the parliament's capacity to act.
- Second, an analyst-type administration offers legal and procedural advice on the options available to parliament. In addition, they could be involved in drafting documents on the basis of debates and in the provision of limited advice – for example, in the form of balanced arguments. This would allow the administration some room to influence parliamentary scrutiny, which could be achieved by highlighting certain possible courses of action. However, the political actors remain in charge of selecting priorities and formulating the actual position through deliberation among themselves.
- Third, the administration could play an advisory role in which its tasks might include the provision of specific content-related advice

(e.g. on whether something constitutes a breach of subsidiarity), which would allow the administration to promote a certain scrutiny outcome. Drafts of opinions and resolutions prior to debates would, of course, also fall into that category of content-related interpretation. These types of activity lead to a certain amount of bureaucratization, but also facilitate improved parliamentary scrutiny by providing MPs with content-related advice.

- Fourth, an administration could play the role of agenda-shaper if it were tasked with the preselection of documents that are particularly relevant for parliament or specific committees. By recommending certain documents for further consideration, the staff would effectively influence the types of issue that are likely to make it onto the parliamentary agenda. Administrations that fall into this category would have the greatest amount of influence on parliamentary scrutiny, and the delegation risk would be accordingly high. On the other hand, the extensive delegation of tasks would allow MPs to process a wider range of issues.
- Finally, a fifth and somewhat distinct role would be that of coordinator. As the EWS and political dialogue are most likely to have an effect if several parliaments push in the same direction, inter-parliamentary coordination becomes increasingly important in the post-Lisbon arrangement. Hence, one can expect parliamentary administrations to play a role in the exchange of information between parliaments on what type of action is being planned by whom. The level of influence depends on the precise tasks: coordination can mean information-gathering, but it could also imply a representational function vis-à-vis other actors in Brussels or 'at home' and, in the extreme, can mean that issues are 'pre-cooked' across national boundaries (Interviews 2, 3, 4).

It is important to note here that the first four roles are likely to be complementary and incremental. In other words, staff playing an advisory role may well also perform the tasks in the categories of analyst and assistant. The fifth role, the coordination function, is set somewhat apart in Table 1.3. It refers on the one hand to inter-parliamentary cooperation and coordination at the European level, and so between two or more national parliaments or between national parliaments and the EP. Moreover, we can also observe this coordination function at the national level, so between the legislature and the executive or between the chambers of a bicameral parliament, for example (Mastenbroek et al. 2014). It has been set apart, because we do not expect this function to be a source of variation in the sense that some parliamentary administrations would have a coordinating role and others not. Instead, we expect that all parliamentary administrations will play a coordination function, also in the context of inter-parliamentary cooperation, but their precise powers and procedures when assuming this role may vary.

The coordinating and cooperative function of national parliaments

In line with the attempts to contribute to democracy in the EU, inter-parliamentary cooperation has been promoted as one possible avenue in order to strengthen the multilevel parliamentary field (Crum and Fossum 2009). Hefftler (2015) sees it as a 'platform to balance intergovernmental decision-making'. The exchange at the transnational level is seen as providing members of national parliaments with insights and information about the interests and the perspectives of MPs from other member states. Given that they are aware of the positions of other member states, the opportunity for MPs to 'assess the governments' win-set in EU negotiations' can allow for better parliamentary scrutiny (Benz 2011, in Hefftler 2015).

While academic attention devoted to inter-parliamentary cooperation in general is growing (Costa and Latek 2001; Crum and Fossum 2013; Herranz-Surrallés 2014; Hefftler and Gattermann 2015), the cooperation between officials and the coordinating function they might assume has, thus far, been missing from the scholarly debate. This can be possibly attributed to the fact that the transnational cooperation of officials is a fairly recent phenomenon. Empirically, we can observe the proliferation of a network of national parliamentary representatives (NPRs) at the European level (see Chapter 3).

In order to better understand the nature of this network of parliamentary representatives, the concept of epistemic communities is instructive, as it has been developed in the context of officials engaging in international policy coordination. Epistemic communities have been described as a 'network of professionals with recognized expertise and competence in a particular domain and an authoritative claim to policy-relevant knowledge within that domain' (Haas 1992: 3). What is crucial is the fact that the professionals making up epistemic communities share normative and principled beliefs, notions of validity, and a set of common practices associated with certain problems and policy issues (Haas 1992: 5; Clemens and Cook 1999: 446).

When applying this to the EU, in the context of the role of government representatives in EU treaty reform, Reh (2007: 1189) adds to these dimensions issue-relevant expertise, experience in negotiating internationally and effective preparation, including access to information on ongoing negotiations. Richardson points to the fact that such networks are important in the EU exactly because they so 'often transcend national boundaries'. The policy community/policy network approach can, in contrast, enhance our understanding of the ways in which agenda issues are channelled into legislative proposals – especially areas of 'low politics' that are of a highly technical nature (Richardson 2006: 6).

However, within epistemic communities its members often 'go native' – that is, their actions are no longer exclusively determined by their principals, but also by a feeling of solidarity with the group. In the EU context, this phenomenon has so far mainly been identified with regard to government officials in Council working groups. Regular meetings between government officials are seen as contributing to the development of a high degree of collegiality and collective identity among officials (e.g. Juncos and Pomorska 2011). Beyers and Dierickx (1998) contend that nationality – while remaining important in many respects – is diluted in the Council, as a supranational network develops in juxtaposition to the intergovernmental characteristics of agents. Checkel (2003) has also found that, in the context of the Council of Europe, social agents go 'native'. A sign of an epistemic community is when officials start to moderate their mandates or develop codes to signal disagreement with their official mandate to their peers on the international level (cf. Beyers and Dierickx 1998; Checkel 2003; Juncos and Pomorska 2011). In Chapter 3 of this book, we apply this concept when analysing the network of NPRs.

While the network of NPRs can be seen as the most established form of transnational cooperation between parliamentary bureaucratic actors at the EU level, other forms of cooperation between officials also exist, such as the cooperation between officials within the COSAC Secretariat. Officials also attend and prepare inter-parliamentary meetings such as Inter-parliamentary Conferences on CFSP/CCDP or the Speakers Conference. These are, however, rather incidental forms of transnational bureaucratic cooperation.

When it comes to the tasks that officials perform in inter-parliamentary cooperation, the information-gathering and -processing activities of the network of NPRs should be highlighted (see Chapter 3). Especially for parliaments with weaker administrative capacity, being informed about files that other legislatures see as controversial can facilitate and enhance parliamentary scrutiny. It is worth noting that the

COSAC Secretariat feeds into the tasks that NPRs perform – for example, through compiling information on parliamentary scrutiny in their bi-annual reports. The COSAC permanent member can be seen as key within the COSAC Secretariat in coordinating the work of the COSAC Secretariat and assisting the COSAC Presidency and the Presidential Troika (see Chapter 3).

Conclusion

In order to fully appreciate the role that parliamentary administrations play in the context of EU affairs scrutiny, one needs not only to understand the range of tasks performed by administrators, but also their potential for administrative influence over outcomes. Towards this aim, this chapter developed a typology geared towards capturing the nuances of the technical and political tasks that parliamentary administrators assume. In fact, we developed two typologies of tasks: one for the EP and another for national and regional parliaments. These are similar in their basic approach but adapted to the specific environment in which officials operate and also reflect the specificities of the different categories of institutions.

One of the main challenges for the EP is to guard and maximize its role in inter-institutional relations. This, in turn, has an impact on the role that officials play within that institution. Moreover, both the technicality of legislation and the complexity of inter-institutional negotiations, especially under the Ordinary Legislative Procedure (OLP), have an impact on the role that officials may assume.

In the case of national parliaments, we see information-processing as a key challenge facing national and regional parliaments after Lisbon. We can therefore expect the tasks of parliamentary administrations to revolve around that challenge. Accordingly, we have developed a typology which distinguishes between technical tasks and more political tasks.

Interviews

Interview 1: Dutch Lower House, VVD MP, 28 March 2012.
Interview 2: French Senate, senior EU clerk, 25 May 2012.
Interview 3: Swedish NPR, 17 November 2010.
Interview 4: Irish NPR, 13 January 2010.

2
Administrative Players in the European Parliament

(Co-authored with Mathias Dobbels)

Introduction

The EP is arguably the institution that has been transformed the most compared with other EU institutions. It has come a long way from an unelected assembly in the 1950s that was merely consulted by the Council, to a directly elected parliament that has achieved co-legislative equality with the Council in over 85 treaty articles.

The EP has represented (European) citizens since the first direct elections in 1979. By way of debating, passing legislation and scrutinizing the work of the European Commission, it is seen as a 'policy-influencing legislature', as it can amend, reject and even propose laws – for example, via reports prepared under its own initiative. The EP can effectively slow down or actually veto legislation. This makes the EP a powerful parliament compared with many other EU member state parliaments, which do not have such prerogatives (Pegan 2015: 70).

As pointed out in the Introduction to this volume, beyond its legislative role, the EP is also a key player in the EU by way of its powers in the appointment of the Commission – which became very apparent in the 2014 elections – and through the adoption of annual budgets and multi-annual financial frameworks.

Moreover, since the Lisbon Treaty entered into force, the EP has had an important role to play in the conclusion of international agreements (Articles 207, 218, the Treaty on Functioning of the European Union [TFEU]). The Parliament's consent is required for almost all international EU agreements (Ripoll Servent 2014). The Lisbon Treaty and the subsequent Inter-institutional Framework Agreement between the Parliament and the Commission ensure that the EP is informed throughout all stages of the negotiations until the international agreement is concluded. Furthermore, the participation of the EP in the process provides the opportunity to propose modifications to the text of agreements.

Since Lisbon, the Parliament has been involved in the conclusion of a number of international agreements that have received much media attention, including the Terrorist Finance Tracking Program (SWIFT/TFTP) and the EU Korea Free Trade Agreement (FTA). In 2012, it declined to consent to the Anti-Counterfeiting Trade Agreement (ACTA) (http://epthinktank.eu/2013).

Taken together, this has led some authors to describe the EP as an 'empowered institution' (Hix and Høyland 2013) and others to see the EP as the 'winner' of the latest constitutional reform by way of the Lisbon Treaty (Lammert 2009).

This extension of powers not only has implications for the directly elected Members of Parliament (MEPs), but also for officials employed by the EP. Moreover, the institution itself has transformed considerably since the 1950s, when the EP was still an unelected Common Assembly with six member states. Officials are currently working within an institution that encompasses 751 directly elected members from 28 member states and that has 23 official languages.

Moreover, ever since the introduction of the co-decision procedure through the Maastricht Treaty, the EP has received significantly more powers. Also, the procedure itself has been transformed considerably (Kasack 2004), both on a constitutional and an informal basis, leading some to coin it as a laboratory for 'institutional innovation and change' (Shackleton and Raunio 2003).

This, we would argue, provides a unique working environment for EP officials, which is also the case when comparing this to the context in which parliamentary officials find themselves working within national parliaments (even when dealing with EU affairs). Both the specific institutional context of the EP and the co-legislative role that the EP fulfils are seen to have specific implications on officials working within that institution. The challenges that EP officials face seem – at least initially – very different from those that administrators deal with when working on European issues within *national* parliaments. On that basis, we would hypothesize that EP officials play a (more) substantial role within this transnational parliament that is characterized by a high degree of turnover of MEPs that carry a substantial 'co-legislative burden'.

This brings us back to the over-arching question that guides this book – namely, how much power administrators possess in order to influence the policy process. For the EP, the more specific question thus relates to the extent to which EP officials can play a role within the EU policy process.

We will answer this question by examining the role of officials in selected cases that fall under the ordinary legislative procedure (OLP), the procedure under which MEPs can exert the most influence over the policy process vis-à-vis the other institutions, in this case the Commission and the Council.[1]

Due to the fact that the OLP has been extended to a large number of policy fields, the underlying question driving this contribution (apart from the more general question raised above) is where MEPs obtain the input and expertise necessary for policy-making and the role played by officials in this context?

In order to be able to operationalize this question, we draw on the roles that have been referred to in Chapter 1. Accordingly, officials could play a 'production role', which implies that they prepare draft reports and meeting documents. The so-called 'service role' would imply that MEPs are briefed extensively on compromise proposals that are to be put forward under the OLP. A so-called 'steering role' would imply that officials would, for example, intervene directly in negotiations with the Council (see Chapter 1).

To complement our analysis, we also focus on the negotiations of an annual budget (specifically, the case of the 2011 budget), which was part of the multi-annual financial frameworks (MFF) for 2007–13. As mentioned, the Lisbon Treaty placed the Council and the EP on an almost equal footing in this domain. Another area where the EP has been 'upgraded' through the Treaty of Lisbon is that of international agreements. However, we did not include the latter in our analysis as the EP plays a very specific role here. It is only informed on the negotiations and, although it can propose modifications, it is in much more of a 'take-it or leave position', as opposed to the OLP. This has led authors to describe the EP as a 'norm-taker' in this field (Ripoll Servent and MacKenzie 2012). For that reason, the role of officials in this domain is likely to be very specific and, as such, does not allow for generalizations. The latter are, however, needed in order to be able answer the broad question framing this chapter and to allow for further comparisons with the role of officials in national parliaments.

Against this background, the structure of this chapter is as follows: first, we provide an overview of the EPs administrative system and then shed light on the growing literature in this field, enabling us to introduce the analytical framework and the case studies. In the concluding section, we try to come to more comparative observations – that is, whether the role EP officials play in shaping EU affairs is larger than that of officials in national legislatures in EU affairs.

An overview of the EP's administrative system

Officials of the EP cannot be seen as a single unit of analysis. Indeed, the political hierarchy in the EP and the transformation from unelected institution to directly elected parliament facilitated the three-tiered structure of administrative machinery: MEPs (individual assistants), political groups (political group staff), and the level of the EP itself (General Secretariat) (Neunreither 2006).

Furthermore, the conditions under which certain civil servants are employed allow us to distinguish between permanent staff, personal assistants, temporal staff and contract agents (Corbett et al. 2011) as follows:

Permanent staff of the Parliament is assigned to the General Secretariat and belongs to the highest level of administrative machinery. The number of officials working in the General Secretariat is estimated to have comprised around 6,700 in 2014 and has grown along with the upgrade of the EP as a co-legislator from around 500 in 1970 (Corbett et al. 2007: 193; EP General Secretariat 2010, Annual Budget 2014) (see Table 2.1).

Figures that are available for 2013, in which the figure is even higher, reflect a more complete and differentiated picture than that given in Table 2.1 because it includes group staff. As Pegan points out, in 2013 the total number of staff working in the EP was 8,308. Within this category, 5,602 were working for the EP's General Secretariat, 1,016 officials supported the political groups and 1,690 worked as assistants.

Note that not all of these officials support MEPs on legislative issues. In fact, less than half of the officials in the Secretariat (2,595) and two fifths of the employees in political groups (415) belonged to the

Table 2.1 Number of civil servants working in the EP

	Civil servants	Officials (Secretariat General)	Temporary agents (Secretariat General)
1970	532		
2003	4,960		
2010		4,497	454
2014		6,743	

Source: EU Financial Report and EP General Secretariat 2010, Annual Budget 2014.

so-called AD category that is responsible for legislative assistance (Pegan 2015: 59).

Two prominent features of the Parliament's nature – multilingualism and geographical dispersion among three cities – have an impact on these numbers. Indeed, one can assume that one third of the Secretariat officials are translators providing official translations of all the Parliament documentation into 23 working languages (Corbett et al. 2007: 193, 2011). Nevertheless, the number of staff that specialize on policy issues, support the sectoral committees and work for MEPs directly is 'unseen in other parliaments of Europe' (Pegan 2015: 16). A much higher number of civil servants thus work in the EP than in national parliament in Europe. Around 2,500 officials work in the administration of the German Bundestag and the French National Assembly employs 1,349 officials (Pegan 2015: 16).

The main tasks of the General Secretariat, according to the EP's webpage, are formulated in rather vague terms: coordination of legislative work, and provision of technical and expert assistance to the parliamentary bodies and MEPs. The Secretariat consists of the Legal Service and nine different Directorate Generals (DGs), and comprises tasks such as communication and finances.

Among the DGs that are pivotal in the process of EU policy-making are the two DGs for Internal and External Policies. The DG for Internal Policies is primarily responsible for the 'smooth running' of the legislative and non-legislative activities of parliamentary committees in the field of internal policies. The DG for External Policies, on the other hand, assists the Parliamentary Committees in the field of Foreign Affairs, Human Rights, and Security and Defence, as well as Development and International Trade. It does so by providing the committees with briefings, background notes and long-term studies on all aspects of Parliament's activities within the domain of internal policies. Some of the main tasks in this context include the provision of expertise in external relations to parliamentary bodies and Parliament's President, and close cooperation with the EU institutions, including the High Representative of the Union for Foreign Affairs and Security Policy (Corbett et al. 2011: 223).

The staff of the EP General Secretariat is subject to the same requirements as civil servants working in other European institutions. According to Article 11 (96) of the Staff Regulations of Officials of the European Communities (2004), 'An official shall carry out his duties and conduct himself solely with the interests of the Communities in mind; he shall neither seek nor take instructions from any government, authority, organisation or person outside his institution. He shall carry out the duties assigned to him objectively, impartially and in keeping with his duty of loyalty to the Communities' (I-8). Corbett et al. (2007) do however point to cases where, at the higher levels (Director and Director-General), appointments are made by the Bureau of Parliament and political factors do play a role alongside nationality, seniority and ability.

Moreover, every MEP has a number of *assistants* at his or her disposal. The status of accredited parliamentary assistants was upgraded by way of a Council regulation in 2009. This implies that assistants enjoy similar social benefits to those of EP civil servants, with their salaries graded accordingly. All contracts automatically end at the end of each legislature. MEPs are entirely free in the selection of candidates they wish to work for them. Typically, between one and three accredited assistants work for one MEP, resulting in a total number of 1,535 assistants in 2011 and 1,690 in 2014 (Romanyshyn and Neuhold 2011; Busby 2013; European Parliament 2014).

Temporal staff of the EP are subject to regulation by the Conditions of Employment of Other Servants of European Communities. While their contracts remain identical to those of permanent staff in terms of rights, working conditions, social benefits and the like, the main difference is that the bond to the administrative posts is not permanent. Their employment may be terminated at any time subject to one month's notice per year of service. According to the Article 8 of the Conditions 'temporal staff [...] shall not be engaged for more than four years [...]. Their contracts may be renewed not more than once for a maximum period of two years.' The majority of temporal posts are filled by political groups.

Contract staff are fixed-term employees who can be employed for a maximum of three years in the Parliament. Their working conditions are different to those of temporal staff and salary scales are entirely different, usually lower, and are related to the amount of professional experience of the applicant (Romanyshyn and Neuhold 2011).

Academic research on the roles of EP officials

The impact of the extension of the Parliament's legislative powers on its internal organization and patterns of interaction between political and administrative players has received little scholarly attention until recently. The debate is gaining ground (Neunreither 2006; Winzen 2011; Egeberg et al. 2013), but there is still a lacuna with regard to the actual impact administrators have on the EU policy-making process.

Neunreither (2006) was the first to examine the role of officials within the EP. He shows how the transformation from unelected assembly to directly elected legislature has provided considerable room for manoeuvre for unelected officials and has had considerable impact on their role – way beyond the introduction of direct elections in 1979.

Scholars have used this work as a stepping stone in order to examine the role of officials working for EP committees. Winzen (2011: 41) addressed the puzzle of whether the work of EP officials has a purely technical dimension or actually has bearing on the policy-process. He comes to the conclusion that under certain conditions, officials who have limited administrative autonomy can be reduced to mere paper-keepers (Winzen 2011: 28).

Egeberg et al. (2013), who probe into the activities of EP staff by way of an online survey (N = 118), observe that these actors rank European issues above national ones and focus mostly on sectoral issues. In institutions such as parliaments where there is a fluctuation among the political elite, administrators could evolve into the institutional memory of the institution (Egeberg et al. 2013: 500). When focusing on what officials actually do in the practical political process – that is, what tasks they (say they) perform – it becomes apparent that providing background information for MEPs ranks at the top of activities, followed by the drafting of documents (Egeberg et al. 2013: 510).

Egeberg (et al. 2014) have also taken up a practice more prevalent within the USA – that is, to investigate whether there is a link between certain characteristics of officials and whether this has an impact on their work. Egeberg et al. (2014) thus probe into the question as to whether factors such as nationality, gender, educational background, organizational socialization and category of staff actually impacts on the behaviour adopted by officials. While a majority of these variables are not seen to have an effect on staff behaviour, both length of service in the EU institutions and type of staff are seen to make a difference. Thus, while recruitment of both EP officials and staff of political groups is generally based on merit, nationality and party membership are identified as additional factors in decisions about the appointment of group staff. In addition, group staff is more likely to emphasize national concerns. This can be explained by the organization of political groups within the EP (Egeberg et al. 2014).

Brandsma (2012) examines the processing of information by the EP and the role administrators play in the context of decision-making in the area of comitology: a complex system of implementing committees staffed by civil servants from the member states and chaired by the Commission, which has been reformed by the Treaty of Lisbon (Christiansen and Dobbels 2013). Brandsma's analysis demonstrates that the assumed link from information to parliamentary behaviour is far from 'automatic'. Transparency itself cannot be seen as the 'magic recipe', as the volume and quality of information that recipients receive is not enough to produce effects. Rather, what is crucial is that the information is *processed*. The crucial question for parliaments to exercise control is, thus, not how much information MEPs receive but the degree to which they (can) actually make use of the available information (Brandsma 2012: 89). Dobbels and Neuhold (2014), when examining the processing of information within the EP General Secretariat, come to the conclusion that the stream of information provided to EP officials is rather far-reaching. This is due to the fact that interest groups provide MEPs and the EP's supporting staff with detailed position papers, analyses and, sometimes, even amendments and voting lists (Dobbels and Neuhold 2014).

In a somewhat similar vein, Marshall (2012) examines the type of advice officials from the General Secretariat provide to rapporteurs, and probes into the question regarding the sources from which this advice is obtained. EP officials are portrayed as generalists that are dependent on the input of lobbyists and even the Commission itself and, as such, indirectly lobby MEPs. Accordingly, Secretariat officials are not independent policy experts but act as 'conduits' for the interests of lobby groups (Marshall 2012). This is increasingly relevant within a parliament that has been upgraded as co-legislator and, by way of the OLP, has been able to 'shape legislation and exercise genuine policy-making power' (Burns 2013: 164).

This ties in with the academic debate on transformation of the co-decision procedure ever since its introduction by way of the Maastricht Treaty more generally. One of the most striking innovations is the opportunity to conclude a legislative file under first reading, also known as the 'fast track'. This procedure was originally meant for technical and/or uncontroversial files but has increasingly been resorted to by both the EP and Council for all types of legislative dossiers (e.g. De Ruiter and Neuhold 2012b; Rasmussen and Reh 2013). The procedure empowers a selected number of players within all three institutions, and within the EP especially, with the role of rapporteur and, as such, engenders the need of bureaucratic support for a number of key players. Increasing inter-institutional cooperation by way of trialogues, involving selected actors from all three institutions, behind closed doors (Burns 2013), not only impacts on the legitimacy of the procedure but could, we would hypothesize at this stage, also affect the role of EP officials.

Overall, the academic debate on officials within the EP only provides limited answers to the question regarding the conditions under which such actors could have an impact on policy-making.

The role of EP officials in the practical political process

From the academic debate on the EP sketched above, we observe that EP officials work in a rather specific context, when compared with officials within national parliaments dealing with EU affairs.

Accordingly we can distil four key features that contribute to this unique working environment:

- Officials have to be able to process very technical legislation under the Ordinary Legislative Procedure within a wide array of policy fields (Burns 2013).
- Officials have to support selected key-players, such as rapporteurs, that are only appointed for the duration of the adoption of specific dossiers, which implies that their 'political masters' change on a regular basis (De Ruiter and Neuhold 2012a).
- The increasing prominence of informal and secluded forms of inter-institutional cooperation that however take place on a very regular basis also might have an impact on the way EP officials work (Rasmussen and Reh 2013).
- Officials work within a transnational parliament that brings together MEPs from 28 member states with a high turnover of MEPs, which contributes to the fact that officials become the memory of the institution (Egeberg et al. 2013).

These features combined lead us to the assumption that EP officials could play a significant role within the EP and one that transcends that of officials working within national parliaments dealing with EU affairs. We put this assumption to the test by studying the work of officials within the EP Secretariat within five different policy fields.

The work of EP officials in practice

The case study design, which covers five cases, is one of 'most different cases' (Peters 1998: 37–41) in order to establish relationships among variables that are valid in a range of different cases.[2] In the case of the EP, this enabled us to trace the internal decision-making process in the EP during legislative negotiations.

An in-depth documentary analysis was complemented with semi-structured interviews.[3] During our research, we covered 'vast ground' by examining the following cases:

- The regulation stipulating the rules and general principles concerning mechanisms for control by member states of the Commission's exercise of implementing powers (thereafter the new comitology regulation). The EU has its own system of conferring powers of implementation from the legislators to the executive. The Lisbon Treaty reformed this system to a certain extent by introducing two new legal bases – namely, Articles 290 and 291 of the Treaty on the Functioning of the European Union (TFEU), respectively dealing with delegated acts and implementing acts. The European Commission put forward its proposal for a regulation on Article 291 TFEU in March 2010 and both legislators came to an agreement by the end of the year. It is the negotiations on this regulation that constitute the focus of the first case.[4]
- The regulation on certain provisions for fishing in the General Fisheries Commission for the Mediterranean (GFCM) is a transposition file whereby decisions of that Commission that fall into the realm of international fisheries are translated into EU law by means of a regulation. Negotiations with the EP started in the first half of 2010, and soon came to a halt on the issue of the use of delegated acts for certain modifications. In the GFCM case, the Council unanimously and consistently pushed for implementing acts and, in some cases, even for amending the regulation through the OLP, rather than supporting delegated acts where the Commission has considerable leeway (Interviews 11, 12 and 13). The EP – in line with the Commission – argued for a broader list of provisions to be amended through delegated acts. A compromise was found in early second reading.
- The negotiations on a new regulation on novel foods. The revision of this dossier is part of a domain that was not affected by the entry into force of the Lisbon Treaty. This thus constitutes an area where

the EP had co-legislative rights before the Treaty came into force. The Commission proposal of 2008 (European Commission 2008) for a revision of the regulation of 1997 included a simplified procedure for 'traditional' food coming from third countries, provisions on foods modified by nanotechnology[5] and the main cause of contention: food derived from cloned animals or their offspring. The EP advocated the total removal of such food from the scope of the regulation, demanded a separate instrument and wanted to introduce a transitional ban for such food being put on the market. After the Council rejected the EP's amendments in second reading, a conciliation procedure was started in early 2011 but failed to reach agreement (Eurofond 2012).

- The negotiations on the long-term residents directive within the field of migration. The directive deals with the status of third-country nationals who are long-term residents in EU member states. Note that the recast aimed to extend the provisions to refugees and other 'beneficiaries of international protection'. Although the subject matter is attributed great 'political' importance by both the member states and within the EP, the adaptation was technically quite simple. In just two trialogues a solution was found (Dobbels and Neuhold 2013).
- The negotiations on the annual budget of 2011, which was part of the multiannual financial frameworks (MFFs) for 2007–13 was the focus of the next case. The Lisbon Treaty placed the Council and the EP on an almost equal footing in this domain, implying that both have to agree on the budget before it can enter into force.[6] The new rules also cut the procedure short by one reading, implying that if the Council does not accept the EP's position on the Commission's proposal or if no common version is agreed after informal negotiations, the text goes straight to a conciliation committee. As in the OLP, this committee is composed of an equal number of representatives of both institutions operates by strict deadlines.[7] Although an agreement on the substance of the budget for 2011 was reached, no agreement was found in conciliation on 15 November 2010. This can be attributed to that the EP demanded to be more closely involved in the future MFF negotiations (for the period 2014–20). Formally speaking, the EP only has the right to assent or disagree with the MFF as negotiated between the Commission and the Council. Eventually, both branches of the budgetary authority could agree during the negotiations in 2010 when the EP was assured that it would be briefed and debriefed by the Council presidency and the Commission

on the MFF negotiations (Neuhold and Dobbels 2014; Dobbels and Neuhold 2015).

In a very legal and technical field such as the negotiations on the design of the system of implementing and delegated acts (former comitology), we could observe that the Secretariat played a role that transcends that of production and service (identified by Page and Jenkins 2005). In terms of the role played by civil servants in the new *comitology regulation*, we came across a close working relationship between EP committee officials and the civil servant working for the political group of the rapporteur. The division of labour between the Secretariat and the group staff was along technical versus political lines, implying that the Secretariat was responsible for most of the drafting of documents and amendments and that the group staff was responsible for the political coordination with the other groups and committees.

The Secretariat has been described as the absolute 'expert in the file', partly because the head of unit of the Secretariat of the Committee dealing with Legal Affairs (JURI) was a member of the working group during the Convention that drafted the two new treaty articles on delegated and implementing acts. Moreover, a close working relationship based on trust resulted in a fruitful cooperation and in a unified position of the EP vis-à-vis the Council. Trialogues were extensively prepared by the Secretariat together with the Presidency at the level of civil servants, with complete agendas – one of which even prescribed which potential compromises would be tabled at which stage of the negotiations. The Secretariat thus had a great impact on the substance of the EP's position, but this was always under the guidance of the rapporteur and his staff. The Secretariat also played an important role in ensuring that all other interested parties in the lead committee (JURI committee) and in the other committees were regularly briefed by the rapporteur on the proceedings of the negotiations with the Council.

In terms of the roles officials performed, we observed that the Secretariat played a role that transcends that of production and service and steered the file without, however, going beyond the instructions and mandate given by the rapporteur (Neuhold and Dobbels 2014).

The reason why the Secretariat had such a considerable impact on the dossier was mainly due to its expertise in the file and its excellent working relationship with the rapporteur and his supporting staff, making this a classic case of 'politicized competence' (development of expertise in fields that officials care about).

We could also observe a similar substantial role played by EP officials in the domain of *fisheries*. The Secretariat of the Fisheries Committee is described as the 'guardian of the EP's rights' in the field of fisheries (Dobbels and Neuhold 2013). After the Lisbon Treaty entered into force, the number of administrators increased from four to eight. In addition to that, two staff members of the Directorate General for Internal Policies of the EP Secretariat were now employed to work full-time on background briefings and studies for the Fisheries Committee. Due to the fact that only a small minority of MEPs has expertise in the domain of fisheries where the main stepping stones are of an institutional nature, EP civil servants are perceived by actors from all institutions to influence the political negotiations substantially (Dobbels and Neuhold 2013). They are even considered as more demanding and less flexible than the MEPs themselves in inter-institutional negotiations.

Within the case of the Regulation on the GFCM, EP officials tried to influence the dossier beyond the instructions of their principals. While both the rapporteur and the representative of the largest political group agreed with the compromise put forward by the Council, the Secretariat intervened during the negotiations and argued against an extension of the list of provisions to be amended through delegated acts.[8] Officials also opposed the conclusion that a deal was found in the preparatory meeting. The rapporteur then followed suit and delayed the adoption of the file for months. It was only in June 2011 that an agreement was found whereby the list was extended as compared with the Council's initial proposal. The Secretariat of the Fisheries Committee thus had a considerable impact on the outcome of the negotiations. The fact that EP officials intervened directly in political negotiations with representatives of the Presidency and with the Commission clearly goes beyond a production or service role (Neuhold and Dobbels 2014).

Yet, even in cases that were attributed high political importance[9] – such as the *regulation of novel foods*, which touched upon the issue of cloning – EP officials still played an important role by determining key organizational aspects, such as the organization of informal negotiations or drawing up compromise amendments. As such, they were able to determine the substance of the dossier, at least to some extent. One has to emphasize that the rapporteur belonged to the far-left European United Left/Nordic Green Left group and that the file therefore required considerable coordination with the other political groups – even more so when it went into conciliation.

The file was, however, characterized by a highly unified position on the part of the EP, mainly on the issue of cloning. It was virtually impossible for a politician to argue in favour of placing food on the market that has any link to cloned animals. Even though the file was thus politicized, the EP was unified and the high degree of political importance attributed to the dossier only aggravated the divergent views between the EP and the Council and the Commission, rather than causing internal conflict. This allowed the Secretariat to play the role of 'guardian' of the EP's position.

In terms of coordination, the Secretariat played a strategic role by always ensuring that, even in informal meetings between the EP representatives and the other institutions, all groups would be either present or at least extensively briefed on the possible compromise proposals to be launched. It did so with the objective of standing strong on the EPs position and not giving in too easily to the Council.

Our observations point towards the fact that, even though the dossier was attributed high political importance, the Secretariat played a key role in defending the position of the EP in inter-institutional negotiations. It did so not only by boasting expertise on the substance, but also by intervening within the organizational aspects of the negotiations. Yet, this was done always in accordance with MEPs and their staff. The Secretariat therefore assumed a role going much further than the mere production of documents, which can be placed between service and steering (Neuhold and Dobbels 2014).

Another case that falls within a field that attributed high political importance is the *long-term residents directive* within the field of migration. In terms of the role of civil servants, we see that they adopt a production role under the OLP. Both rapporteurs in charge on behalf of the Socialists and Democrats (S&D) seem to have been very involved in the negotiations, often directly contacting the respective actors in the Commission and the Council. In terms of preparation of the draft texts, the assistant of the respective MEP was 'teamed up' with the respective official from the Secretariat. Both trialogues were prepared on a technical level by the rapporteur's assistant, the Secretariat and a representative of the Council, after which the shadow rapporteurs were consulted. All the major political groups were generally supportive of the rapporteur's approach and open to go for a first reading agreement. The drafting of the report and preparation of the trialogues were based on a very clear mandate from the rapporteur, but the bulk of the work in terms of writing the report and preparing the trialogue was done by the Secretariat.

Due to the fact that it was a relatively consensual file in the Parliament in political terms, the Secretariat was responsible for most of the drafting of compromise amendments.

The case of the *budget of 2011* is somewhat special in terms of staff involvement as it is a case in which practically the entire EP is involved. A significant majority of committees have to give their input to the budgetary committee, which takes the lead in the negotiations with the Council. Political group staff and EP committee officials can be said to have played a very substantial role in the negotiations. Contrary to the case of comitology, where coordination took place on a more informal and ad hoc level, the system in the budgetary procedure is highly formalized. Group coordinators are vital in this respect. They meet in committee and negotiate among themselves before submitting amendments to the lead committee. Group staff thus takes on an important preparatory role in scrutinizing each amendment. Apart from the group staff, EP committee officials can also be ascribed a key role in preparing the trialogue negotiations and drafting official documents. Apart from the head of unit, one EP official is assigned to each budget heading respectively. The tasks to be performed range from following coordination meetings, making calculations and drafting briefing notes to collecting amendments and drafting voting lists. By having built up a relationship of trust with the committee chair, EP officials can rely on the necessary political backing.

Due to the highly formalized procedure and the fact that the file was attributed high political importance, the role of EP committee officials was reduced to production; this consisted of the compilation of amendments, assisting the rapporteur with her draft report and drawing up voting lists. There was no room for manoeuvre for substantial input by EP committee officials as the main negotiations were carried out by coordinators, who were assisted by group staff (Neuhold and Dobbels 2014).

Analysis and concluding remarks

Our analysis reflects that a combination of three factors can create the conditions under which officials can play a key role under the OLP and, as such, contribute to the shaping of policy within the EP:

- Officials must invest in developing their expertise within subjects and dossiers that are of interest to them – that is, possess what Gailmard and Patty (2007) describe as 'politicized competence' (see Chapter 1).

- The political importance attributed to a certain dossier within the EP also has an impact on the role played by officials. Interestingly, although officials can play an important role in files that are attributed low importance, their role can also be key in dossiers that are attributed high political importance, such as the dossier on novel foods.
- A high degree of consensus within the EP – that is, a somewhat unified position – across political cleavages within the EP moreover contributes to a situation where EP officials can play an important role.

These empirical observations feed into the conceptual debate on parliamentary bureaucratic systems insofar as the roles developed for administrative players within ministerial bureaucracies can only be applied to a limited extent (see Chapter 1). We can thus observe that, under certain conditions, EP officials assume a role that transcends the respective conceptualizations (Page and Jenkins 2005).

In certain dossiers, such as the file on the reform of comitology, we could thus observe that officials played a role which we have classified as a *steering role*. This implies that EP officials substantially influence the relevant dossier or the actual negotiations and, as such, contribute to shaping policy outcomes. This might come as no surprise in this very legal and technical field of the system of implementing and delegated acts, where we could observe that the Secretariat played a role that transcends that of production and service. As has been alluded to above, officials steered the file – but, however, without going beyond the instructions and mandate given by the rapporteur.

Yet, even in cases that were attributed high political importance such as the regulation of novel foods, which touched on the issue of cloning, EP officials still played an important role by determining key organizational aspects, such as the organization of informal negotiations or drawing up compromise amendments. As such, they were able to determine the substance of the dossier, at least to some extent. The Secretariat thus assumed a role that can be placed between that of service and steering. Not only did the officials possess 'politicized' competence, but also the file was characterized by a highly unified position on the part of the EP, mainly on the issue of cloning. It was virtually impossible for an MEP to argue in favour of placing food on the market that has any link to cloned animals. This made it easier for EP officials to defend the EP's position, as the latter was crystal clear.

Note that, as far as we could observe, the steering role EP officials adopt is linked to the preservation of the institutional prerogatives of the EP. The politicized competence that EP officials gain within this transnational legislature is thus indeed not 'neutral' in the Weberian sense but expertise that is linked to preserving the EP's position in inter-institutional bargaining.

This leads us to answering the question raised at the outset of this chapter: to what extent can EP officials play a role within the EU policy-process? We have observed that in more technical dossiers, such as the reform of comitology, and also in cases such as placing novel foods on the market or in the field of migration EP officials can contribute to the shaping of policy.

What is very crucial for questions of representation, is that we could not observe a case where directly elected members of parliament did not have the last call, i.e. did not take the final decision. One has to stress that these decisions are increasingly taken behind closed doors, secluded from the public eye during early stages of policy-making.

Let us now put the role EP officials play within the EU policy-process into a larger context and compare it with that of officials working within national parliaments. Overall, EP officials seem to play a greater role than national parliamentary officials in EU affairs.

In our research on officials in national parliaments, we distinguish between five different types of staff roles: administrative assistant, analyst, advisor, agenda-shaper and coordinator (see Chapter 5). It is interesting that even the analyst who provides concrete solutions and drafts also, prior to debates in selected national parliaments, seems to have less impact on the *substance* of the dossiers than EP officials under the novel foods dossier or in the domain of fisheries, for example. The most extreme case is the one of the GFCM regulation, in which EP officials intervened directly in political negotiations with representatives of the Presidency.

This variation in roles can be attributed to the fact that the contexts in which officials find themselves working differ widely. The role of national parliaments in EU affairs is more restricted if you compare it with the role that the EP plays within the EU multi-level system; it is, after all, a fully-fledged co-legislator with the Council in a large number of policy domains. Moreover, the transformation of the EP from consultative assembly, with members delegated by national parliaments, to a directly elected institution is generally seen as contributing to the fact that officials traditionally have had a considerable room for manoeuvre (Neunreither 2006).

The fact that the EP is a much more heterogeneous institution than national parliaments, with a high turnover of MEPs dealing with highly technical legislation on a very regular basis, also contributes to the fact that officials can take on a considerable role. Moreover, the complexity of (inter-institutional) negotiations leads to a situation where officials have to provide technical-substantive assistance, such as providing procedural and legal advice (Pegan 2015: 83).

Overall, our general observations fall in the category of 'optimal delegation' (see Chapter 1). Legislative delegation can be desirable if 'agents' carry out the tasks delegated to them by their principals in line with the original mandate issued (Boehmke et al. 2005). Within the EP, we can thus observe that officials do not constitute a 'runaway bureaucracy' but that they contribute to 'optimal' policy solutions.

Interviews

Interview 1: with a representative of one of the member states, Brussels, 7 February 2012.
Interview 2: with a representative of one of the member states, Brussels, 22 February 2012.
Interview 3: with an official from one of the EU institutions, Brussels, 16 March 2012.
Interview 4: with an MEP, Brussels, 13 April 2012.
Interview 5: with an MEP, Brussels, 16 May 2012.
Interview 6: with an official of the EP, Brussels, 3 May 2012.
Interview 7: with an official of the EP, Brussels, 16 May 2012.
Interview 8: with an official of the EP, Brussels, 17 May 2012.
Interview 9: with an official of the EP, Brussels, 24 May 2012.
Interview 10: with an official of the EP, Brussels, 25 May 2012.
Interview 11: with an official from one of the institutions, Brussels, 12 May 2011.
Interview 12: with an official of the EP, Brussels, 27 May 2011.
Interview 13: with a representative of one of the member states, Brussels, 14 April 2011.
Interview 14: with an official of the EP, Brussels, 2 May 2011.
Interview 15: with an official from one of the institutions, Brussels, 10 June 2011.
Interview 16: with an official from one of the institutions, Brussels, 24 June 2011.
Interview 17: with a representative of one of the member states, Brussels, 13 March 2012.
Interview 18: with a representative of one of the member states, Brussels, 17 April 2012.

Interview 19: with an official from one of the institutions, Brussels, 12 December 2011.
Interview 20: with an official from one of the institutions, Brussels, 6 August 2012.
Interview 21: with an official of the EP, Brussels, 26 July 2012.
Interview 22: with an official of the EP, Brussels, 31 October 2012.
Interview 23: with an official from one of the institutions, Brussels, 25 April 2012.
Interview 24: with an official of the EP, Brussels, 31 October 2012.
Interview 25: with an official of the EP, Brussels, 19 October 2012.

3 Transnational Bureaucratic Networks in the EU: The Role of Parliamentary Officials in Inter-Parliamentary Coordination and Control

Introduction

The pressure for national parliaments to cooperate systematically with one another and the need to develop a high level of technical and legal expertise (see Chapter 1) have led to the growth of a network of permanent representatives of national parliaments (NPRs) to the European Union. These are (unelected) officials that are dispatched by their respective national parliaments to Brussels for a certain period of time. Despite the fact that this network has rapidly expanded – it now encompasses representatives from almost all 28 national parliaments,[1] with some bi-cameral parliaments sending two representatives – it has received little academic attention. The number of NPRs has not diminished, not even during the economic and financial crisis; in fact, the number has consistently expanded since 1991. Even the parliament of a non-EU member state, Norway, now has a representative in Brussels.

This network can be seen as the most far-reaching form of transnational cooperation between parliamentary bureaucratic actors at the EU level, but other forms of cooperation between officials also exist, such as the cooperation between officials within the COSAC Secretariat.[2] While the main focus of this chapter will be directed towards the network of NPRs, this will be put into context by comparison with other forms of transnational bureaucratic cooperation, such as officials working within the COSAC Secretariat.

Methodologically, this chapter builds primarily on a series of semi-structured interviews conducted with NPRs.[3] This data has been supplemented by interviews with officials working within parliaments in the national capitals and the results of a survey of experts working on national parliaments.[4] Moreover, interviews have been conducted with officials working for the COSAC Secretariat.[5] By way of this data collection, all EU member states have been covered, at least to some extent.[6]

Against this background, this chapter is structured as follows: we first give an insight into the network of NPRs before then comparing it with officials working in the COSAC Secretariat, and shedding light on other forms of inter-parliamentary cooperation involving officials. We go on to examine how bureaucratic networks can play out in the political process by illustrating the way in which the first two 'yellow cards' in the EWS were issued. The chapter closes with concluding remarks.

The network of national parliamentary representatives: Rationale and tasks

The development of the network of NPRs over time

The roots of the network of NPRs can be traced back to the early 1990s as the Danish national parliament, the Folketing, sent a representative to Brussels in 1991.[7] At the time, it was the first legislature to deal with EU issues rather intensively by way of its mandating rights of the respective minister in the Council. This delegation of a parliamentary representative to Brussels thus 'came rather naturally' (Interview 4). The rationale behind this decision to send a parliamentary administrator to the European arena can be explained by the fact that it was seen as necessary to be able to develop a parliamentary stance and position independent from the Danish government. The aim was thus to assist the Danish Folketing in exercising its powers of parliamentary scrutiny.

The Finnish parliament then also sent a parliamentary official in 1995, with the same objective: to obtain first-hand information not provided by the executive (Interview 7). Italy followed suit in 1998 by sending an NPR to Brussels part-time, which required the representative to commute from the Italian capital. The UK House of Commons delegated an official the following year.

A significant influx only took place prior to and after the 2004 enlargement (cf. Figure 3.1). However, this 'boom' was only partially related to enlargement insofar as it also included 'older' member states

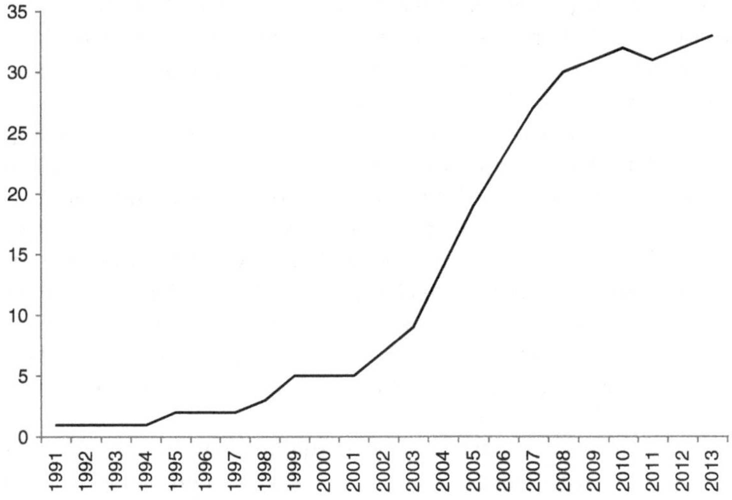

Figure 3.1 Total number of NPRs per year (including both upper and lower houses)
Source: Compilation by authors.

such as Germany, Greece, Belgium, the Netherlands and Austria (lower chamber). The last member states that sent a representative were Malta and Croatia in 2012 and 2013, respectively. Norway, as a member in the European Economic Area, has sent a representative since early 2013.[8]

Thus, the network has grown even in times of financial crisis, where one can assume that there has been pressure on administrative expenditure. This can be seen as a reflection of its perceived added value. In fact, the House of Lords is currently considering a recommendation from the UK government to increase the number of British NPRs in Brussels before the next British Council Presidency (House of Lords 2014) and the Dutch parliament has recently decided to appoint two NPRs instead of one (Interview 14).

Close ties to the sending institution

One feature that all NPRs have in common is that they are experts in parliamentary affairs. They are, for the most part, direct delegates of their parliament and are in constant contact with their 'home parliament'. Parliamentary representatives are officials of their respective parliament and most have worked within their legislature for several years prior to having been dispatched to Brussels. It is seen as vital that the NPRs have close ties to their respective national parliament in order to draw on established contacts with both officials and MPs and also to know 'what matters' (Interview 23).

As systems of parliamentary control are not only rather complex, but also have their unique ways of functioning (O'Brennan and Raunio 2007), it is key that an NPR is aware of how the relevant political system works and which players are responsible for which type of issues at which stage of the policy-process. Is the sectoral committee or the European affairs committee in charge? If the plenary has to take the final decision, the scrutiny process takes longer and the NPR needs also to factor that in. The Dutch and Danish NPRs, for example, tend to update the relevant committees regularly when the respective parliament is aiming for a yellow card (Interviews 25 and 26).

A large number of NPRs – such as the Spanish, Italian, Portuguese, Austrian, Swedish, Finnish, Danish and Dutch representatives, as well as those of the French National Assembly and of the UK House of Commons – maintain their ties by going back to 'their' member state parliament on a monthly basis. In this context, the prime objective is that of information exchange – conveying developments from the EU arena to the national level and vice versa. NPRs attend staff meetings of officials working for sectoral committees and the EAC, and provide reports on EU affairs (Interview 21).

Several NPRs see their respective committee responsible for European Affairs (and, where relevant, the Secretariat General) as their 'primary clients' (Interviews 15 and 17). However, there is a trend that, in member states that have joined the EU more recently, this direct 'relay function' has been reduced or replaced with other means of communication. After assuming her function in 2008, the Lithuanian NPR initially went back home every six months, for example. After the Eurozone crisis, most of the contacts now take place via email, phone and videoconference. The same is true for the permanent representative of the Polish Sejm, who also keeps in touch mainly via email with the Polish parliament (Interviews 16 and 17).

In general, the socialization in the home parliament is strong, with the effect that the NPRs form a group marked primarily by *national* ties and mandates. Most NPRs are recalled after a few years to return to work within their respective national parliament. They thus keep their allegiance to their national parliament, as their career prospects are determined by the perception of their performance by national actors.

Key tasks: Information exchange and representation?

What is key for the way NPRs conceive of their role is the fact that they see themselves as neutral players and professionals that have, in some cases, passed entrance exams and are regularly dealing with technical issues (Interviews 1, 11, 15, 20 and 22). Thus, instead of developing a set of joint beliefs and common views on substantive issues, NPRs are usually requested not to engage in substantive debates. The work of NPRs tends to be based on formal 'mandates' or parliamentary positions, such as parliamentary or committee resolutions and opinions. These officials are thus cautious when it comes to interpreting content (Interview 20; Monday Morning Meeting, 6 May 2013). Rather, the core task is to 'build networks, especially with other parliaments and to find out what they do and alert them to what we do' (Interview 24). Thus, the close ties with the national legislature in combination with a reluctance to engage in substantive debates have a threefold effect on the role of NPRs.

NPRs maintain close contacts within the respective national parliament in order to obtain information: they know where to turn when trying to obtain first-hand information on sectoral issues, but also have insights on possible violations of the subsidiarity principle. Their function is being described as being the 'eyes, ears and mouth' for their respective parliament and, as such, to function as an 'information-relay' or 'information-broker' for their respective legislature (Interviews 10, 15, 16, and 23; Bill Cash 2013).[9] The familiarity of NPRs both with staff and members of parliament also ensures a high degree of trust and familiarity, and enables them to adopt a parliamentary stance and position on EU affairs (Interviews 15 and 17).

Due to the fact that NPRs are all located on the same corridor of the EP (except for the German delegation and the Belgian NPRs),[10] they are in a perfect position to gather more informal insights regarding the stance on specific issues taken within other parliaments or developments at the EU level (Interview 26). If one is in need of specific information or the position of a respective legislature on a specific issue 'you just go down the hall' (Interview 16).

The second – and related – task of the NPRs is to assist their respective parliament in exercising democratic control (Interview 15). This not only implies the forwarding of information, but also that NPRs assume a key role in *information-processing* – that is, identifying and framing what could be relevant for the respective national parliament. The Commission sends a large number of documents to parliaments and NPRs contribute to the identification of issues that are to be subject to parliamentary control. In this endeavour, information has to be 'tailor-made to parliament's needs' and is required to show an awareness of the priorities of the parliament (Interview 23; Pinheiro 2012: 212). In parliaments that select priority dossiers for scrutiny, it is the NPR that keeps bilateral contacts with sectoral committees and assists them in the selection of priority dossiers for parliamentary scrutiny (President of the Portuguese Parliament 2008).

In addition, the task of NPRs is to alert their respective parliament to the general stance taken by national parliaments on a specific dossier, especially when a greater number of parliaments are starting to discuss the adoption of reasoned opinions on a certain issue. The Danish NPR, for example, informs his parliaments of all reasoned opinions submitted by other parliaments long before they are published in the official database IPEX (Interviews 25 and 27). Especially under the EWS, where parliaments are actually aware that a minimum number of opinions has to be reached, there is a 'bandwagon effect' that gains momentum in the final weeks. By keeping their parliaments abreast of such dynamics and of the objections of other parliaments, NPRs can to some extent frame their parliament's agenda (Interviews 24, 25 and 26).

NPRs act not only as a platform of information exchange *across* national parliaments when coordinating 'yellow cards', but also as a forum for the exchange of best practices in parliamentary control. In this vein, they exchange views – for example, on the functioning of the system of mandating the executive in other member states in order for national parliaments to enhance their scrutiny systems.[11]

Third, the work of the NPRs also has an important 'European' dimension and, as such, contacts to the three main institutions involved in EU policy-making are seen as crucial (Pinheiro 2012). Both the EP and the Commission are seen as main players in this context. The link to the EP is facilitated by the fact that a majority of NPRs are based within the premises of the EP. The network with the Commission spans all layers of the European executive (Bauer 2009); European Commission officials, members of *cabinets* and Commissioners. As a result, not only Commission officials, but also Commissioners themselves attend the meetings of NPRs (Interview 5). The normal duration of the regular Monday Morning Meetings of the NPRs has thus increased from a few minutes in 2008 to between two and three hours in 2014, as the NPRs are now also inviting Commission officials and – to a lesser extent – Council representatives to join these meetings (Estonian NPR, 31 March 2014).

A rather novel development is the fact that parliamentary representatives seek systematic contacts with their respective permanent representations. While some NPRs such as the French even have an office in their permanent representation, in other member states these contacts are in the process of being intensified (Interview 21). Contacts to the Conference of Parliamentary Committees for Union Affairs of Parliaments of the European Union (COSAC) are simplified by the fact that the COSAC Secretariat is located within the same building as the NPRs and also because COSAC representatives attend the regular meetings of the NPRs. Moreover, NPRs from the relevant parliaments are part of COSAC during the period their institution is part of the Troika.

COSAC, as will be explained, is thus seen as an internal rather than external partner, with NPRs being seen as an 'excellent source of information' (Interview 5). In this endeavour, NPRs are described as a 'bridge between Brussels and the parliaments in the capitals' (Interview 29).

NPRs also play a role in reflecting on a possible reform of COSAC meetings, in order to enhance parliamentary influence. Currently, there are discussions on developing COSAC meetings' 'new style', along the following lines: more discussion of substance – for example, of certain policy-dossiers, more opportunities for informal exchange between MPs and staff, and more opportunities to influence the agenda by other parliaments than that holding the Presidency (Mastenbroek et al. 2014). These issues were, inter alia, discussed between NPRs and representatives of the COSAC Secretariat.

However, despite these contacts with the EU institutions such as the Commission, the representative function of NPRs towards these bodies is rather weak. The main aim of encounters with Commission or Council representatives tends to be directed towards information-gathering, rather than the representation of a legislative position (Interview 24).

When NPRs are involved in the *representation* of national parliaments at the European level, this is mostly in a supporting function. On the one hand, NPRs provide support to their parliamentary president and to the delegations of their respective parliament when attending meetings of the EU institutions and collaborate in the organization and following-up of work and study visits by members and parliamentary officials to the European institutions (Interviews 21 and 10). On the other hand, the 'relay function' with regard to their national legislature also implies that NPRs accompany EU representatives such as the President of the EP or Commissioners when visiting their respective parliament and attending plenary or committee meetings (Interviews 17 and 15).

Now that we have shed some light on the network of NPRs, we will put this into context by comparing it with other forms of interparliamentary cooperation involving officials.

The role of NPRs in context: A comparison with the COSAC secretariat

The COSAC Secretariat has, inter alia, been set up to promote inter-parliamentary cooperation. In this vein, the COSAC Secretariat has as its goal the assistance of COSAC in its endeavour to further the 'exchange of information and best practice between national Parliaments and the European Parliament, including their special committees'.[12]

COSAC itself, which is a Conference of the European Affairs Committees of national parliaments as well as representatives of the European Parliament, was established in May 1989. According to the Lisbon Treaty, COSAC may also organize inter-parliamentary conferences on specific topics – in particular, within the field of common foreign and security policy (CFSP). It is noteworthy that the Treaty of Lisbon stresses explicitly that COSAC has a supporting role vis-à-vis national parliaments as 'contributions from the Conference shall not bind national parliaments and shall not prejudge their positions'.[13] COSAC has a role in 'show-casing' the importance of the rotating Presidency of the EU as COSAC meetings usually take place in the capital of the member state holding the Chair.

As Hasters (2014) points out, a notable development in COSAC's history was the setting-up of a permanent Secretariat. This had been on the COSAC agenda repeatedly and had been rejected time and time again – in 1995, 1997 and 1999 (COSAC 2013a). The necessity for a secretariat grew as the European Affairs Committees (EACs) of the Presidency could not face the organization of the COSAC meetings alone (Tordoff 2000: 4). It was in 2003 that, finally, a permanent Secretariat of COSAC was created. When it comes to the composition of the COSAC Secretariat, the rules of procedure of COSAC clearly make a link to the EU rotating Presidency by stipulating that 'the COSAC Secretariat shall be composed of officials from the Parliaments of the Presidential Troika'.[14] Moreover, the COSAC Secretariat is to have a permanent member who supports the Secretariat in its activities (European Parliament 2011: 9.1, in Hasters 2014).[15]

Note that the actual size of the COSAC Secretariat varies: while some Troika parliaments send one representative, others send more than one. It is thus up to the relevant national parliaments to decide who they actually appoint as members of the Secretariat. Additionally, in some cases the respective officials wear 'two hats', insofar as they hold the position of the NPR of the respective member state and, at the same time, assume the position within the COSAC Secretariat. Other national parliaments send one official solely for the tasks in the Secretariat. This implies that not only does the composition of the COSAC Secretariat change with each new Presidency, but also its capacities (Hasters 2014). Moreover, a representative of the EP in charge of relations with national parliaments is represented in the Secretariat. This member changes on a regular basis (Interview 29).

This position does, however, not compete with that of the permanent representative within COSAC.[16] Due to the fact that he or she is appointed for two years, with a possible renewal for a further two, this representative can be seen as being in a key position compared with the other members of the Secretariat. The process of appointing the permanent member of COSAC is based on the COSAC Rules of Procedure. Accordingly, the permanent member is appointed by the COSAC Chairpersons on the proposal of the Presidential Troika. It is noteworthy that it is a formal precondition that the permanent member is an official of a national parliament (Interview 29). Moreover, the permanent member is very often also an NPR prior to the appointment to the COSAC Secretariat, which is seen as being very useful, as one permanent member of the COSAC Secretariat points out:

> I was already acquainted with the multi-national Brussels' environment, the multi-faceted work required here; inter-parliamentary affairs and with colleagues from other parliaments (national parliaments and EP) and other EU institutions. I also had the opportunity to be a member of the COSAC Secretariat itself;[17] of the Troika of COSAC and to work closely with its Permanent Member and with other Troika colleagues. The fact that before that I had been working in the European Affairs Service of a national parliament supporting the Committee on EU affairs was also useful.
>
> (Interview 29)

The permanent representative assumes somewhat the role of the memory of the institution due to the fact that he or she is based in Brussels for around three years and plays a key role behind the scenes of COSAC. As such, the representative obtains a comprehensive and comparative overview of the actual role different national parliaments assume in the scrutiny of EU affairs, especially when compiling the COSAC reports (Interview 5). In spite of being a national official, the permanent representative serves all of COSAC during his or her term, and not primarily their own parliament.[18]

The main tasks of the COSAC Secretariat, as such, are stipulated in the Rules of Procedure (RoP 9.4):

> The COSAC Secretariat shall assist the Presidency Parliament in all its tasks. The members of the COSAC Secretariat shall perform their duties under the political responsibility of the COSAC Presidency and the Presidential Troika or according to the decisions taken by COSAC meetings. The Permanent Member shall coordinate the activities of the COSAC Secretariat under the direction of the Presidency Parliament.

Against this background, the concrete tasks of the Secretariat can thus be grouped into two main categories in the practical process: secretarial/organizational issues related to (COSAC) meetings and drafting COSAC documents.

Secretarial/organizational issues related to (COSAC) meetings: The COSAC Secretariat provides assistance, support and advice to the Presidency Parliament by way of organizing the meetings of the COSAC Chairpersons and the COSAC plenary and, as such, takes care of any organizational issues related to these tasks. The COSAC Secretariat does not assist in preparing the Conference of Speakers.

Drafting COSAC documents: The bulk of the work of the Secretariat of COSAC meetings consists of drafting documents, such as the COSAC bi-annual reports. The drafting of the bi-annual report is based on Parliaments' replies to a questionnaire sent to Parliaments (national Parliaments and the EP) on certain topics to be covered in the bi-annual report. The COSAC Secretariat collects the replies and draws up a synthesis (Interview 19). COSAC has published such bi-annual reports on EU practices and procedures since 2004 and these give an insight into developments at the EU level and parliamentary practices in the member states (Hefftler and Gattermann 2015). In this way, COSAC officials contribute to the coordination and dissemination of information, and adopt the role of coordinator (cf. Pegan and Högenauer in press). Moreover, the COSAC Secretariat assists the Secretariat of the Presidency Parliament in preparing the documents for the COSAC meetings. It is the COSAC Secretariat that also drafts the minutes of the COSAC meetings. Note that *within* the COSAC Secretariat the workload is divided/distributed among the members of the Secretariat on the basis of a proposal by the permanent member who coordinates the activities of the Secretariat (Interview 19).

As has been mentioned, there are close ties with the permanent representatives of national parliaments. Depending on the workload,

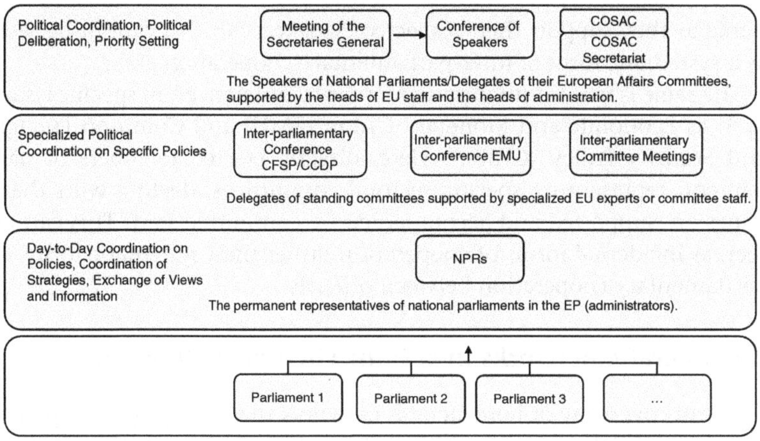

Figure 3.2 Parliamentary administrations in inter-parliamentary cooperation

officials of the COSAC Secretariat may attend Monday Morning Meetings. Also NPRs may attend COSAC meetings – according to the internal arrangements of each national parliament – and be able to 'follow what is going on'. The information exchange goes thus both ways (Interview 19).

As is apparent from Figure 3.2, COSAC are not the only form of inter-parliamentary cooperation that involves officials, at least to some extent. The oldest form of inter-parliamentary cooperation is the 'Conference of Speakers of the Parliaments of the EU' which held its inaugural meeting in Rome in 1963. Since 1975, they have met on an annual basis (before that, only irregularly). The Conference consists of the speakers of national parliamentary chambers and the President of the EP. Similarly to COSAC, each Conference is chaired by the speaker or president of the parliament which holds the EU Presidency during the second half of the calendar year.

Within the framework of inter-parliamentary activities, the Conference of Speakers regards its own central functions as to safeguard and promote 'the role of parliaments and carrying out common work in support of the inter-parliamentary activities', to represent a 'forum for the exchange of opinions, information and experiences among the Speakers' and to 'oversee the coordination of inter-parliamentary EU activities' (Article 2, see Conference of Speakers, 2010, in Hefftler and Gattermann 2015). In this form of inter-parliamentary cooperation, senior officials (heads of EU staff and heads of EU administration) play a role as they support their respective speakers but this cannot be seen as a systematic form of inter-parliamentary cooperation.

The same is true for Inter-parliamentary Conferences on specific issues such as Economic and Monetary Union (EMU) and Common Foreign and Security Policy (CFSP).[19] Here, directly elected members of parliament, representing specific sectoral committees, dealing with these issues are supported and accompanied by committee staff. This can be seen as incidental forms of cooperation rather than systematic forms of parliamentary cooperation between officials.

Bureaucratic networks in action: The two 'yellow cards'

After this overview of bureaucratic networks that bring together parliamentary officials, we wish to show how these operate in the practical political process leading to the first two 'yellow cards' issued in the context of the EWS. Here, the main focus is on the network of NPRs in the role of coordinator (as outlined in Chapter 1) but we also touch on the involvement of COSAC.

In practice, the network of NPRs can be useful in three ways: it meets on an almost weekly basis on Monday mornings.[20] As a result, it is the only forum of inter-parliamentary cooperation where parliaments can exchange information on a legislative proposal regularly and in a timely manner against the backdrop of the tight eight-week deadline to submit a reasoned opinion (Interviews 3, 11, 13 and 27). As a Belgian clerk working within the Belgian parliament stated:

> The NPRs are generally quite important in the subsidiarity procedure, not just for Monti II (the first yellow card). It is from there that national parliaments and their administrations get timely information about the intention of other parliaments to adopt a reasoned opinion.
>
> (Interview 27)

National legislatures can be alerted to the fact that one or more legislatures are planning to conduct a subsidiarity check even before the Commission formally comes up with a proposal (Interview 13).

Second, the meetings allow parliaments to gather additional information from Commission officials by way of presenting an upcoming proposal, for example. Third, the meetings focus on selected priority issues that are of relevance at a given time; such as the European semester and the implications thereof for national parliaments. The agenda items for the Monday Morning Meetings are tabled in accordance with the representatives of the network of NPRs (informally known as the 'group'). In order to be able to prepare these meetings effectively and to become a 'one-stop shop' both for the network and for outside stakeholders, NPRs have chosen to appoint informal coordinators. At the time of writing, three coordinators were appointed by their peers, chairing the Monday Morning Meetings in rotation and sharing out their tasks among themselves. Each of these coordinators is responsible for a different dimension of inter-institutional cooperation.

The role of the NPRs in the process that lead up to the adoption of the two 'yellow cards' illustrates how the network functions and what relevance it has for parliamentary control.

The 'first yellow card' was issued on the so-called Monti II regulation,[21] which was meant to clarify the right to organize collective action. On 21 March 2012, the Commission proposed two draft texts, an implementing directive clarifying the implementation of the 1996 rules (that were in force until then), and a regulation concerning the right to take collective action in situations that have a cross-border dimension (Petitjean 2012). The proposed regulation immediately met with harsh opposition from trade unions and employers' organizations. During the eight weeks after the proposal was published, 12 national parliaments (19 votes) raised the issue that the proposed regulation violated the principle of subsidiarity and issued reasoned opinions, which lead to the first 'yellow card'.

The role of the NPRs in Monti II was twofold. In the first instance, the Danish parliament used their NPR to mobilize other parliaments. The Danish parliament had already put Monti II on its list of priorities for subsidiarity control as it was likely to have an impact on the Danish welfare system. It was thus able to react promptly in formulating a reasoned opinion within the first few weeks after the proposal was submitted. It was seen to be a concise but clear statement of the main concerns and was made available in English. The Danish NPR played a very proactive role and circulated the Danish reasoned opinion as a 'blue-print' among the network of NPRs in order to encourage other legislatures to follow the Danish example (Interviews 25 and 26).

In this context, it is interesting to note that the close link between COSAC and the NPRs was also apparent in this first yellow card. Coincidentally, Denmark also held the COSAC presidency and the meeting of the delegates of European Affairs Committees was well-timed. The Danish EAC chair could thus use that meeting to push further for reasoned opinions among directly elected members of Parliament (cf. Christensen 2015) even if, at that point, most of the coordination work had already been done (Interview 25).

The network of NPRs then built on the catalyst effect of the increasing number of opinions. Momentum was created by informing all national legislatures of additional reasoned opinions that were being put forward, thus raising interest in an increasing number of national parliaments (Interviews 24 and 27). The Dutch decision to adopt a reasoned opinion on the last day of the deadline, for example, was probably in part motivated by the fact that achieving the necessary threshold for the 'yellow card' was within close reach (Interview 26). The example reflects the fact that an insight into the proceedings *en grand* can trigger action and lead to concerted outcomes that could otherwise not have been achieved (Cooper 2013; House of Lords 2014). The Danish EU advisor observed, 'I am not sure if there could have been a yellow card without the NPRs' (Interview 25). Similarly, as the time-frame of eight weeks is so extremely tight, an NPR shares this view:

> IPEX does not give you informal information; not that type of information that is exchanged on the sixth floor. We did not open a bottle of champagne on our floor after the first yellow card but it was apparent that this was very much because of our work.
>
> (Interview 15)

The second yellow card was reached on the proposal regarding a European Prosecutor Office in 2013. In this case, the Dutch were crucial as the dossier had already been earmarked as a priority issue on the basis of the Commission work programme a year in advance. Thus, the Dutch NPR raised awareness about the publication of the proposal and notified the other NPRs about the intention of the Dutch parliament to issue a reasoned opinion. She also proactively informed the network of the Dutch activities on the dossier and asked for information on the stance of other legislatures. Here, the Dutch also benefited from the interest of other active parliaments (Interview 26).

Overall, the two examples thus further illustrate how bureaucratic networks can play out in the practical political process. Especially, NPRs by way of functioning as administrative spokespeople for their parliaments can thus facilitate the attainment of common solutions.

Conclusion

Overall, we see that officials can play a key role in inter-parliamentary cooperation. Here, the network of NPRs can be seen as central. The network contributes to the attainment of common outcomes that could otherwise not be achieved by working as an information relay both *towards* their respective national legislatures and *across* national parliaments. It is in the very nature of the Lisbon provisions that a certain degree of coordination between national parliaments is needed in order to raise subsidiarity concerns. In practice, this coordination takes place to a large extent on the bureaucratic level. Officials, in turn, direct the attention of decision-makers to issues that might be of political importance.

The review of the background and tasks of NPRs leads us two observations. On the one hand, NPRs share a common background and have a high level of expertise. On the other hand, their ties to their sending institution, to their respective national parliament, are very close and remain very close throughout their time in Brussels. Despite their similar background, they thus remain primarily 'national agents' with a past and future in the service of the national parliament. A look at the tasks of the NPRs highlights information-gathering and interpretation for the national level as their main role, followed by the facilitation of contacts with the European institutions and other Brussels actors. The representational function of parliamentary representatives is, however, comparatively weak. While they facilitate the attendance of political members of national parliaments in important fora and may inform other actors about the position of their parliament, the NPRs see themselves as administrators who are clearly not to negotiate, deliberate or decide on behalf of their parliaments.

NPRs generally emphasized the importance of committee/plenary positions as a basis for action, as well as their close ties to their respective parliaments. The career structures of parliamentary officials generally give credibility to such claims, as NPRs usually return to their parliaments after a couple of years and pursue a career in the domestic context. Finally, our analysis has reflected that NPRs proactively embrace subsidiarity scrutiny and parliamentary activity under the EWS and thus, in general, identified strongly with the mandate of their principals.

The extensive information-gathering and -processing activities of the network are designed to facilitate political scrutiny. Especially for parliaments with weaker administrative capacity, being informed about the dossiers that other legislatures find problematic can facilitate and sharpen parliamentary scrutiny. In addition, the fact that most NPRs see their future within their parliament and have closely knit ties facilitates political control.

When comparing the network of the NPRs with other forms of inter-parliamentary cooperation between officials, we see that this network has become an important institution. The COSAC Secretariat also consists of parliamentary officials but, even then, there is a strong link with the NPRs as these are, in selected cases, part of the Secretariat. It is noteworthy that the COSAC Secretariat, in turn, feeds into the tasks that NPRs perform – by, for example, compiling information on parliamentary scrutiny by way of the bi-annual reports. The role of the COSAC permanent member, who has to be an official of parliament and very often has assumed the role of NPR of his/her respective parliament, is of paramount importance within the COSAC Secretariat. He or she coordinates the work of the COSAC Secretariat, works somewhat as a memory of the institution, and plays a key role in assisting the COSAC Presidency and the Presidential Troika.

Noteworthy is the fact that the permanent member of the COSAC Secretariat does not work for a specific national parliament. Although he or she is a parliamentary official and, as such, has parliamentary expertise, he or she has to adopt a transnational parliamentary stance by working for the rotating Presidency. The same is true for officials working for the COSAC Secretariat as a whole. They are delegated from different national parliaments and support the rotating Council Presidency parliament in exercising its tasks. National interests thus move to the back-burner.

Comparatively speaking, the role of officials at the Conference of Speakers is not as far-reaching. Although high-level parliamentary officials attend these meetings, these contacts are more incidental when compared with officials working in the COSAC Secretariat or the representatives of national parliaments in Brussels. The same is true for officials assisting MPs in inter-parliamentary cooperation.

In sum, bureaucratic networks of officials can be seen to play an important role in the context of parliamentary control of EU affairs.

When trying to categorize the roles that officials play within bureaucratic networks according to the categories drawn up in Chapter 1, we see that both NPRs and COSAC officials assume the role of coordinator but to varying degree. As the examples of the two yellow cards have shown, NPRs can play a key role in coordinating activities under the EWS. Moreover, they can play a role in exchanging experiences of best practice of parliamentary scrutiny across national boundaries by way of seminars or informal information exchange. This function of exchanging information across member state parliaments is further enhanced by officials working for the COSAC Secretariat – for example, by way of the

COSAC bi-annual reports. Here, the key aim is the coordination and dissemination of information and best practice across national parliaments and to a wider audience.

Officials working within transnational parliamentary bureaucratic networks – and here, NPRs are the prime example – can, under certain conditions, contribute to concerted outcomes across member state parliaments, by way of information exchange.

Interviews[22]

Interview 1: with a Permanent Representative to the EU, 14 September 2010.

Interview 2: with the administrators of the European Affairs Committee of a national parliament, 27 September 2010.

Interview 3: with a Permanent Representative to the EU, 29 October 2010.

Interview 4: with a Permanent Representative to the EU, 9 November 2010.

Interview 5: with a Representative of the COSAC Secretariat, 9 November 2010.

Interview 6: with a Permanent Representative to the EU, 10 November 2010.

Interview 7: with a Permanent Representative to the EU, 16 November 2010.

Interview 8: with a Permanent Representative to the EU, 16 November 2010.

Interview 9: with a Permanent Representative to the EU, 16 November 2010.

Interview 10: with a Permanent Representative to the EU, 17 November 2010.

Interview 11: with a Permanent Representative to the EU, 22 November 2010.

Interview 12: with a Permanent Representative to the EU, 22 November 2010.

Interview 13: with a Permanent Representative to the EU 17 December 2010.

Interview 14: with a Permanent Representative to the EU 24 May 2012.

Interview 15: with a Permanent Representative to the EU, 24 January 2013.

Interview 16: with a Permanent Representative to the EU, 24 January 2013.

Interview 17: with a Permanent Representative to the EU, 25 January 2013.
Interview 18: with a Permanent Representative to the EU, 25 January 2013.
Interview 19: with a Dutch EAC clerk, 9 January 2012.
Interview 20: with a Permanent Representative to the EU, 7 February 2013.
Interview 21: with a Permanent Representative to the EU, 13 January 2010.
Interview 22: with a Permanent Representative to the EU, 13 January 2010.
Interview 23: with a Permanent Representative to the EU, 25 January 2013.
Interview 24: with a Dutch EU advisor, 16 April 2014.
Interview 25: with a Danish EU advisor, 15 April 2014.
Interview 26: with a Dutch committee clerk, 18 April 2014.
Interview 27: with a Belgian committee clerk, 23 April 2014.
Interview 28: with Permanent Representative to the EU, 25 June 2014.
Interview 29: with a Member of the COSAC Secretariat, 29 January 2015.
Intervention of Estonian NPR at the OPAL Conference in London, 31 March 2014.

4
The Administrations of National Parliaments and the Scrutiny of EU Affairs

Introduction

In the academic literature on parliaments, as in the public debate, the main focus is usually on the party political dimension of parliamentary work: the adoption of legislation or annual budgets, the election and scrutiny of the executive and their important role in the political system as a forum for debate on key issues. Yet, in order to function as institutions and exercise their functions, parliaments also rely on administrative structures and appointed officials.

Parliamentary administrations provide a wide variety of services, involving units such as the secretariats of committees, legal services, research divisions, library and archival staff, advisors to political groups and assistants to MPs. While most of these services are usually classed as 'technical', many of the tasks carried out by administrators have either a strong political dimension or the potential to affect parliamentary decision-making (cf. Gailmard and Patty 2007).[1] At the very least, the quality of work provided by parliamentary administrators contributes to the effectiveness of legislatures, and thus also impacts on their relative strength vis-à-vis the executive and other institutions.

Recognizing the potential significance that parliamentary administrations have, this chapter seeks to illuminate the support that appointed officials provide with the scrutiny of EU affairs. Given the growing complexity of EU affairs and the greater role that national parliaments have gained in the process, the demand for EU-related expertise within parliaments has grown. This chapter focuses on the analysis of the *administrative capacity* of national parliaments in the area of EU affairs. The following section examines the main questions surrounding the role of unelected officials in the context of an elected chamber. In the subsequent section, we then present and discuss the findings of empirical research on the administrative capacity of parliaments across the EU. This is based on data that was collected in the context of the OPAL project, including a survey of EU staff in parliamentary administrations, interview data from 12 EU member states and the chapters of the *Palgrave Handbook on National Parliaments and the European Union*, which contain information on all individual parliaments in the EU (Hefftler et al. 2015).[2] In addition, we have made use of the data contained in the 20th COSAC bi-annual report (COSAC 2013b). The chapter concludes by highlighting the ways in which parliamentary administrators can have an impact on the handling of EU affairs within and among the national parliaments, while also highlighting the limitations they face in carrying out their duties.

Dimensions of administrative support in national parliaments

The field of action of 'parliamentary administration'

In discussing the tasks that parliaments tend to assign to officials, a distinction needs to be made between those officials who work for parliament as a whole – or for one of its chambers, in bicameral systems – and those assigned to a specific committee secretariat. With regard to the former, there are usually a number of officers that legislatures employ in order to provide general support for the work of their elected members, and that might have special significance in the case of EU affairs. Chief among these are legal officers, who provide opinions and advice on legal and constitutional matters. In the area of EU affairs, where there are often uncertainties about the legal dimension of EU initiatives and proposals, such advice is important and potentially influential. Given that one key aspect of the scrutiny of EU affairs is to check whether EU legislative proposals are in conformity with the principle of subsidiarity – a principle that is frequently contested – the advice that a parliament's legal service provides is important in deciding whether to raise objections.

A related role is played by research divisions, which can be asked to produce studies about particular topics on the parliamentary agenda. This often goes hand in hand with legal advice, but can also be of a broader nature – for example, by providing comparative studies on parliamentary activity in other countries or in-depth research on issues on a parliament's legislative agenda. While some such research remains in the realm of advice, some parliaments have set up units – such as the

Bundestag's Büro für Technikfolgen-Abschätzung (TAB) or the European Parliament's Science and Technology Options Assessment (STOA) – to do more far-reaching work on the impact of legislative proposals. To the extent that such reports are made available not only within the parliament, but also to the wider public, the parliamentary research divisions can also be seen as de facto think-tanks engaging in the public debate on topical issues. At the other end of the spectrum is research that is purely meant for in-house use, such as the 'confidential enquiry service' provided by the British House of Commons Library. Libraries are actually maintained by most legislatures for the benefit of members and staff, but some – such as in the UK – also carry out studies, engage in research and provide policy advice.

All the information given above refers to support staff working for the parliament as a whole (unless, in bicameral systems, each chamber maintains a separate unit of this kind). A different set of civil servants is engaged in supporting the work of individual committees – something that is usually much closer to the actual legislative workflow and therefore also of a more narrow nature. Each parliamentary committee is usually supported by a secretariat that includes administrators assisting committee members in the conduct of their business. This ranges from logistical support and procedural matters – management of relations with ministries, the other chamber (in bicameral systems) and other actors – all the way to providing or commissioning policy advice when it touches on substantive issues in draft legislation. Most crucial perhaps, in terms of its political relevance, is the work done by administrators in the interstices between the procedural and the substantive: the advice provided during negotiations, the setting of agendas for meetings between MPs and representatives of the executive, or the search for agreement among different political parties on a committee. While having to remain neutral in party-political terms, secretariat officials can potentially have a significant impact on the outcome of legislative negotiations by the way in which they handle their dossiers and manage the process.

These observations raise the question of politicization – that is, the extent to which administrators working in the service of parliaments may, or may not, be involved in politics. The standard expectation is that, as civil servants, parliamentary administrators must remain neutral. However, the very fact that they 'serve many masters', be they MPs in the plenary or members of a specific committee, and that these are by definition associated with a particular political party, creates an environment in which neutrality becomes a complex issue. On some issues, such as civil rights or climate change, there may be a received wisdom on what parliament's line is but, in many cases, such views will shift with the changing majority following a general election.

It is important to note here that parliamentary administrators work in a matrix-style system in which they are, on the one hand, part of a formal bureaucratic hierarchy, with line managers and, ultimately, led by a secretary-general. Within this system the usual notions of a Weberian bureaucracy ought to apply – a state of affairs that makes the secretary-general an important appointment subject to particular scrutiny when it comes to neutrality (cf. Goetz 2011; Greer and Jarman 2011).[3] He or she will work closely with the Speaker of the parliament, to whom he or she is ultimately accountable.

On the other hand, administrators also work closely with the elected members, be they in the legal or research division (producing specifically requested reports) or in the committee secretariats. With regard to the latter, there is a parallel line of responsibility as administrators work for the committee members and especially for the chair of the committee, and this situation is bound to create circumstances in which party political preferences (majority versus opposition parties) influence the expectations of the inputs by administrators. Here, just as in the context of executive bureaucracies, latent tendencies for politicization are present (e.g. Manley 1968; van der Meer and Dijkstra 2011).

It is the MPs, the committee chairs and the speaker who will have the final word on the formal position of parliament and, as such, the influence of parliamentary administrators will always be limited. Inasmuch as legal advice, research input, policy recommendations or the management of the legislative process – all activities of which administrators are commonly in charge – provide opportunities for agenda-setting, officials can have an influence, at least on setting the agenda if not on the final outcome. In view of the limitations on the time and expertise of elected MPs, this puts the spotlight on the administrative needs of the legislature. Against this background, there is considerable demand for the expertise of administrators, which in turn heightens their potential to influence the policy process, and therefore also the scrutiny of EU affairs. Before looking at the role of administrators in this process in detail, it is useful to explore the nature of parliamentary scrutiny in general.

Political oversight in national parliaments

Through the various tasks outlined above, administrators in most parliaments actively participate in the scrutiny process at several points

Table 4.1 Parliamentary oversight over executive bureaucracies

	Ex-ante (prevention)	**Ex-post (correction)**
Statutory	• Tight laws • Reauthorization bills • Budget	• Budget
Non-statutory	• Politicized appointments	• Hearings • Reports • Appeal to courts
Admin. rules and procedures	• On consultations and stakeholder hearings	• On transparency • On appeals

Source: Compiled by the authors based on Arnold (1987), McCubbins and Schwartz (1984) and Huber (2000).

during the legislative process. There is, however, with the exception of occasional case studies such as Manley (1968), very little literature on the interaction between MPs and parliamentary administrations, and how these are involved in, and supervised during, the decision-making process. As noted in Chapter 1, scholars have conducted research on parliamentary oversight in the US Congress over several decades, and have produced valuable concepts and insights – albeit in the context of parliaments exercising oversight over *executive* agencies – that is, officials who are external to the functioning of parliament itself. The main types of parliamentary oversight over executive bureaucracies that we developed earlier are summarized again here in Table 4.1.

The literature on how the US Congress controls agencies and bureaucrats in executives is not directly applicable to political oversight of administrators in EU national parliaments. In fact, many of the statutory and non-statutory instruments are either too specific, too formal or would backfire. The main difference is that political oversight in the case of agencies is about controlling administrators as they implement and manage procedures after parliament has adopted a policy. In the case of parliamentary staff, it is about controlling administrative activity that *precedes* parliamentary decisions. Parliamentary staff members are usually involved in the preparation of a parliamentary decision, not in the long-term management of policies. The use of laws and reauthorization bills or administrative rules on appeals, transparency and stakeholder hearings only makes sense in the context of policy-related activity where decision-making is delegated to bureaucrats. Hearings with one's own staff would be an overly formal approach and both budgetary instruments and the appointment of politicized staff would backfire in the context of parliamentary administration. In the case of the former, budget cuts to punish or constrain rebellious staff would effectively deprive politicians of their own support. Politicized appointments may work in the case of politically homogeneous governments, but parliamentary administrators are generally expected to respond to all parties, so politicized staff would only generate and reinforce conflicts.

Overall, the instruments available for political oversight of parliamentary administrations are therefore somewhat different. In order to avoid conflict, the parliaments of EU member states generally try to keep parliamentary staff politically neutral and at the service of all parties, while also appointing experts to party groups and personal assistants to MPs. As a result, ex-ante measures on political neutrality and transparency in the work of civil servants are particularly important. In addition, instead of politicized appointments as a non-statutory measure, *non-politicized appointments* become an attractive instrument. In France and Belgium, for example, parliamentary administrators are recruited through a *concours*, and French law imposes strict neutrality requirements on civil servants (Baron 2013; Interviews 1 and 2).

In addition, in the case of legislatures, ex-post correction of administrative behaviour is simpler and functions without cumbersome formal procedures. As all final decisions are taken either in committee or in the plenary, MPs can simply ignore administrative advice and drafts at that point, sideline administrators who are seen as biased, circumvent parliamentary staff with the help of group staff or personal assistants or, in extreme cases, restructure the administration. After all, administrative staff can only be as influential as legislators allow them to be (DeGregorio 1994: 2; Winzen 2011). It is arguable, however, that political oversight is much more difficult to achieve for small, minority parties than for majority parties. As political oversight relies de facto on MPs having the last word, it can be very difficult for opposition parties to hold an administration in check if it is biased and has the support of the majority (cf. Manley 1968).

Political oversight in EU affairs largely relies on the simple fact that decisions are ultimately taken by politicians, not by administrators. The final decision on whether a document is in breach of subsidiarity lies with the relevant committee or the plenary, and what a minister should or should not say in the Council of Ministers is also agreed during committee debates. As a result, administrators need the *trust* of politicians if they want their advice to be translated into concrete actions. The principle of neutrality plays an important role in establishing this trust. In a few cases – such as France, Belgium or Luxembourg – the perception of neutrality is based on recruitment exams that are seen as establishing a system of meritocracy (Baron 2013; Spreitzer 2013). In other cases, the principle of neutrality is enshrined in law or can be derived from constitutional provisions (e.g. Sweden and Portugal; Hegeland 2015; Jančić 2015). In a third group of countries, there are no legal provisions that demand neutrality, but there is a strong professional ethos that political beliefs should not be expressed while exercising one's function as civil servant (e.g. Dutch Tweede Kamer, Interviews 3 and 4). The parliamentary representatives in Brussels, in particular, emphasized the importance of following committee and parliamentary instructions closely (Monday Morning Meeting, 6 May 2013).

In general, the relationship between administrators and MPs is a harmonious one. The interviewees from the 12 case study countries mentioned few instances of disagreement between administrators and MPs beyond the fact that, occasionally, an issue is added to or removed from the list of recommended priority issues. Interestingly, the most frequently voiced concern of administrators seems to be the fear that what they recommend might not be taken up because of a lack of interest in the scrutiny of EU affairs on the part of politicians. The view of Belgian committee clerks is, for example, that the Treaty of Lisbon had little impact on their parliament because Belgian politicians were too pro-European to have a sustained interest in objecting to EU legislation under the EWS (Interviews 1 and 2). Similarly, French clerks expressed the view that some committee chairs did not view the EWS as desirable (Interview 5). Romanian clerks feel that MPs in their committees are not always as interested in certain EU issues as they are themselves (Interviews 6 and 7). Thus, the predominant constraint on administrative activity might in practice be the limitations that administrators face in getting MPs to take up the issues that have been raised. One of the few cases where the relationship between staff and politicians is perceived as problematic is the Czech Republic, where administrators feel that the fact that the government does not have a majority in the Senate has led to increased inter-party rivalry which, in turn, has resulted in increasing pressure on clerks to take sides (Hrabálek and Strelkov 2015).

Parliamentary administrations in EU affairs scrutiny

The organization of administrative support

Just as there is wide variation in the practice of scrutiny of EU affairs by national parliaments (Neuhold and Smith 2015), there is also considerable variation regarding the involvement of parliamentary administrations in such scrutiny. Previous research has only scratched the surface of this topic and the precise implications of the differences between parliamentary administrations remain an open question (Högenauer and Neuhold 2013; Christiansen et al. 2014). One of the greatest sources of variation is the amount of administrative resources at the disposal of a parliament and their organization. Figure 4.1 illustrates the significant differences between the chambers in terms of the absolute number of staff employed in EU affairs, ranging from 1 member of staff to 44.5 members in the case of the German Bundestag.

It might be assumed that the number of EU staff is determined by the size of the chamber – that is, that the Bundestag has the most staff members because of the number of MPs they have to advise. However, Figure 4.2 shows that staff numbers are not always proportional to the number of MPs. Even taking the size of the chamber into account, some chambers have a much larger bureaucracy than others. The German Bundesrat is particularly well-staffed with a rate of just about five politicians per EU staff member. By contrast, the Spanish parliament and the Slovenian National Assembly are outliers with particularly low staff levels: a Spanish EU expert, for example, has to support on average over 100 MPs.

Overall, despite some differences between parliaments, there is a noticeable correlation between the size of the chamber in terms of the number of MPs and the number of EU experts employed by the chamber. The Pearson Correlation Coefficient for these two variables is fairly strong at a level of .66, and the relationship is highly significant (0.000). The remaining differences in relative staff numbers are not easily explained. They do not appear to be directly related to the wealth of the member state or the country-specific impact of the economic crisis. The list of comparatively well-staffed chambers includes, for example, those of Cyprus and Romania. Similarly, one cannot blame a lack of motivation for comparatively low levels of staffing. Sweden has the third highest number of MPs per EU expert, but its parliament generally appears to be a high-performing scrutinizer of EU affairs (Auel et al. 2015a).

In addition, parliaments with larger administrations tend to have more EU experts than parliaments with small administrations. As could be expected, these two variables correlate quite strongly, with an R^2 of 0.69 and a significance of 0.000. However, as the overall parliamentary administrations become larger, the number of EU experts increases quite slowly. In a linear regression equation, the regression coefficient is 0.01, which means that for every additional 100 staff members that a parliament has, it only has one additional EU expert (on average). There are

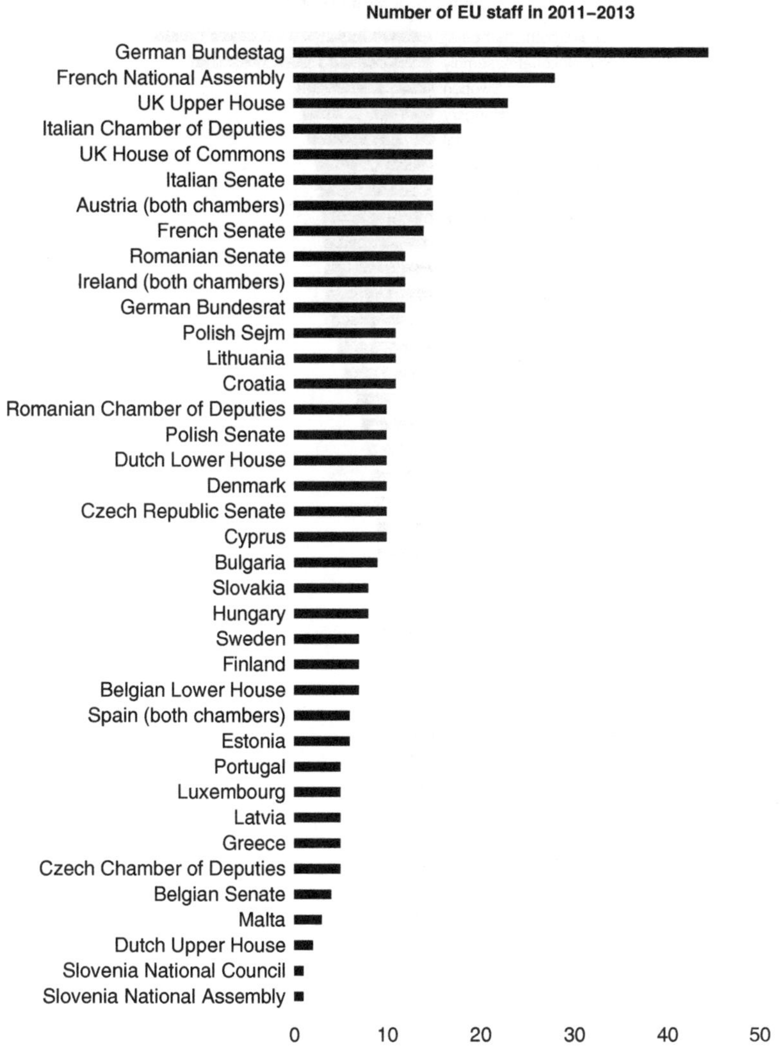

Figure 4.1 Total number of EU staff per chamber (2011–13)

Source: Questionnaire to the EACs of the 27 parliaments and OPAL Country Reports (2012), http://www.opal-europe.org/index.php?option=com_content&view=article&id=94&Itemid=128.

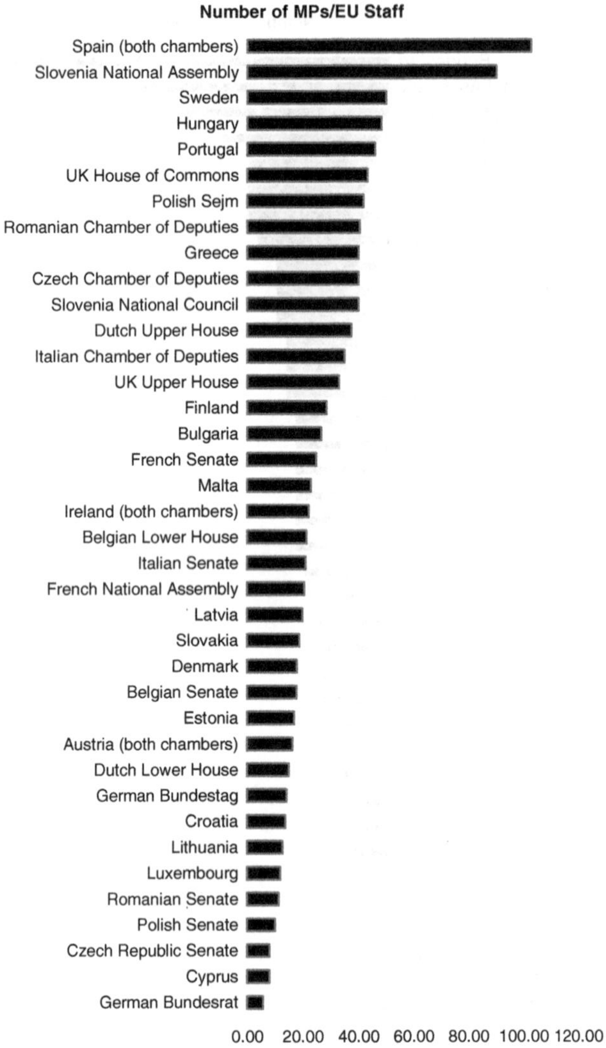

Figure 4.2 Number of EU staff per chamber (2011–13)

Notes: Numbers include all EU staff employed by the chamber, including EAC staff, the EU staff of sectoral committees, research and legal staff, central units, and so on. When calculating the number of MPs per member of EU staff, the official number of seats in the chamber was used. The data thus do not take into account variations in the number of MPs per chamber over time due to vacant seats or temporarily higher numbers due to specific election rules (e.g. the German 'Uberhangsmandate'). Where bicameral parliaments share their EU staff, the MPs of both chambers were added and divided by the number of EU staff.

Source: Questionnaire to the EACs of the 27 parliaments and OPAL Country Reports (2012), http://www.opal-europe.org/index.php?option=com_content&view=article&id=94&Itemid=128.

only five chambers that have four or fewer EU experts: Two of these are in the smallest member states (the Slovenian Chamber of Deputies and the Maltese parliament), and three chambers are relatively weak upper houses (the Slovenian National Council, the Dutch Upper House and the Belgian Senate). This may indicate that a certain amount of staff is seen as necessary to ensure effective EU affairs scrutiny.

At the same time, the slow increase in EU experts beyond that point suggests that there may be a perceived effect of 'diminishing returns' – that is, that parliaments feel that the additional benefits of more staff members start to diminish above a certain threshold of necessary staff. The reason for this could be that the number of EU experts should ideally correspond to the level of interest in EU affairs in the national parliament. If a parliament has a great number of excellent EU experts, it can produce excellent reports on EU matters. But if the MPs of that chamber have a very moderate interest in EU affairs, these reports might never be used in practice. Thus, increasing the supply of expertise makes most sense when there is a demand for expertise among the political masters.

In general, this trend also becomes apparent in the scatterplot in Figure 4.3. In line with the low correlation coefficient, parliaments with a small administration in general tend to have a relatively high proportion of EU experts. However, as the size of the overall administration increases, the share of the EU experts among it drops. Those parliaments that have a low proportion of EU experts tend to have somewhat higher overall staff numbers. Among the 18 cases for which we have data on general staffing levels and for which this relationship could be studied, the UK House of Commons is an extreme example of the trend, whereas the German Bundestag is the only clear outlier.

However, it is important to remember that the nature of staff support depends not only on numbers, but also on quality. The Czech Parliament, for example, has an average level of staff support, with 10 staff, and is further supported by a Parliamentary Institute of eight staff, but is negatively affected by high turnover rates. Thus, an average member of the EU staff there is about 30 years old and has only three years of work experience. The same problem of frequent staff changes applies to the Parliamentary Institute (Hrabálek and Strelkov 2015).

EU experts in changing times

In recent years, parliamentary administrations have faced resource pressures that simultaneously encourage change in two opposite directions. On the one hand, the powers of national parliaments in EU affairs have

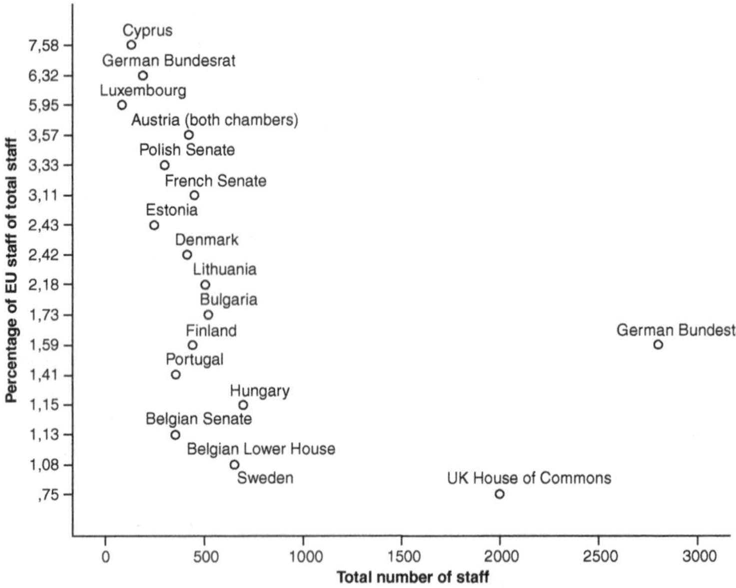

Figure 4.3 Percentage of EU staff among total staff compared with total staff numbers

Source: Parliamentary websites, questionnaire to the EACs of the 27 parliaments and OPAL Country Reports (2012), http://www.opal-europe.org/index.php?option=com_content&view=article&id=94&Itemid=128.

increased over time, allowing parliaments to play a more active role. The Treaty of Lisbon, in particular, has improved the information rights of national parliaments and has created a new role for them in EU policy-making with the opportunity to review the compliance of EU policies with the principle of subsidiarity. In addition, in anticipation of the new treaty, the Barosso Initiative has allowed national parliaments to send substantive comments on new policies directly to the Commission as part of a 'Political Dialogue'. These new powers have 'whet the appetite of national parliaments' for more active scrutiny, and can thus be expected to have increased the demand for bureaucratic expertise in the form of assessments of policies by the parliaments' own administrations. Similarly, the increased flow of information should have increased the demand for administrative expertise in identifying the most important policy documents. From this perspective, one would thus expect higher investments in bureaucratic expertise on the part of national parliaments.

However, at the same time, the financial crisis and later Eurozone crisis have revealed severe budgetary problems in a number of member states which are under pressure to curb public expenditure. Even member states that are not at the heart of the crisis had to cope with slowing economic growth (or no growth) and have thus faced a situation that was hostile towards unnecessary expenditure. These developments therefore create a disincentive for investments in parliamentary bureaucracies, as such investments would run counter to public saving measures.

In the face of these contradictory pressures, we were interested in observing how parliamentary administrations – and especially their EU staff – have evolved since the mid-2000s. As data on the mid-2000s had to be collected retrospectively, it was difficult to obtain this information. For those 15 cases where data could be obtained retrospectively, the combined number of EU experts rose from 144 to 165.5 between 2006 and 2011–13 (cf. Figure 4.4).

While it thus seems, at first glance, that the Treaty of Lisbon had a more important effect than the Eurozone crisis, a closer look at the individual cases shows that the picture is in fact more diverse (cf. Figure 4.5). In reality, five cases out of 15 experienced no change during that time span (Bulgaria, Sweden, Estonia, the Czech Chamber of Deputies and Portugal), although Sweden soon afterwards equipped almost all standing committees with committee officers specialized in EU affairs (Written reply 1). Only six cases employed more EU experts in 2011–13

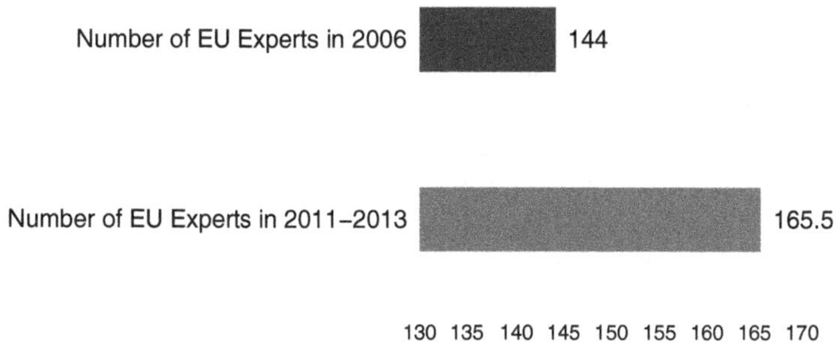

Figure 4.4 Combined number of EU experts in 2006 and 2011–13

Note: The statistic is based on original data on 15 chambers and/or parliaments: the Austrian parliament (which share an administration), both Belgian chambers, the Luxembourg parliament, the Portuguese parliament, the Czech Chamber of Deputies, the Estonian parliament, the Swedish parliament, the Finnish parliament, the Bulgarian parliament, both German chambers, the UK House of Commons, the Cypriot parliament and the French Senate.

Source: Questionnaire to the EACs of the 27 parliaments.

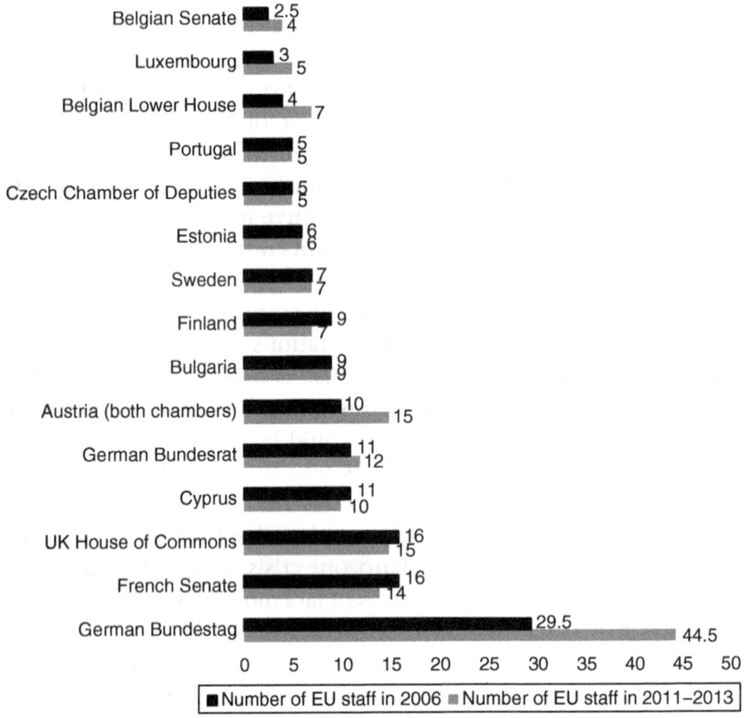

Figure 4.5 Number of EU staff in 2006 and 2011–13
Source: Questionnaire to the EACs of the 27 parliaments.

than in 2006. The biggest changes took place in the Austrian parliament (an increase from 10 to 15 staff) and the German Bundestag (from 29.5 to 44.5 staff). The German Bundesrat, the Belgian Senate, the Luxembourg parliament and the Belgian Chamber of Deputies increased their EU staff by one to three staff members. However, there are also four cases where the number of EU experts diminished over time. The UK House of Commons and the Cypriot parliament reduced their EU staff by one, whereas the French Senate and the Finnish parliament reduced their staff by two.

The reductions in staff are mostly explained by reference to cuts to the parliamentary budget in general and are thus implicitly or explicitly linked to the financial crisis. The Cypriot parliament did not offer an explanation for the staffing cuts, but the European Affairs Committee of the French Senate explained the reduction of staff by reference to cuts to the parliamentary budget (Written reply 2). The Finnish parliament pointed out explicitly that:

> The Finnish administration, including the Eduskunta, committed in 2008 to a programme of austerity, in view of the beginning financial crisis and Finland's long-term fiscal outlook. For the Eduskunta this means broadly that for every two staff members retiring or resigning, there will be only one replacement. Thus staffing levels have generally fallen during the reporting period.
>
> (Written reply 3)

Similarly, the European Affairs Committee of the House of Commons explained that the Treaty of Lisbon had not led to an increase in staff because:

> One administrative staff member was lost due to an overall programme of staffing cuts across the Committee Office. Otherwise post-Lisbon work has been incorporated into the responsibilities of existing staff.
>
> (Written reply 4)

Conversely, the increase in staff in the six cases was partially explained by reference to the increased powers of national parliaments. Thus, the Austrian parliament recruited new staff for the Austrian presidency of the Council of Ministers in 2006 and kept this staff as there was then an increase in the tasks and scope of scrutiny (Written reply 5). The Belgian House of Representatives created a new unit of three staff to analyse the incoming documents and draft subsidiarity opinions (Written reply 6). In the case of the German Bundestag, the increase was in part related to the new powers foreseen in the (failed) Draft Constitution for Europe, but also to a large extent triggered by the Federal Constitutional Court's critical assessments of the level of scrutiny conducted by the German parliament (Written reply 7). In addition, Sweden has recently considerably increased its staff capacity further when almost all standing committees received a committee officer responsible only for EU affairs (Written reply 1).

It has to be noted though that the Belgian Senate, the Bundesrat and the Luxembourg parliament did not increase their staff specifically because of Lisbon (Written replies 8, 9 and 10). Especially in the case of the smaller chambers and parliaments (Luxembourg, the Belgian Senate), the increase may have been more generally due to the fact that their previous staff resources in EU affairs were extremely low.

Overall, it seems that both the Treaty of Lisbon and the Eurozone crisis have affected the staffing policies of national parliaments as regards EU affairs experts. Many parliaments seem to have reacted either to one or the other pressure depending on their perceived need for improved scrutiny or the perceived need for budgetary austerity. In some cases, the budgetary pressures may have curtailed the capacity of parliaments to become more active in European affairs at a time when new opportunities for participation were opening up.

The organization of EU experts

There are differences not only regarding the numbers, but also in terms of the organization. Some parliaments rely exclusively on their EACs to scrutinize EU affairs, while others have mainstreamed this activity and rely primarily on their sectoral committees (see Gattermann et al. 2015). Yet others use a mixed system where the EAC and the relevant sectoral committee both influence the final decisions of parliament. Similarly, some chambers concentrate their staff in the EAC secretariat, some give their sectoral committees independent resources and yet others have a central unit, research unit or legal unit responsible for all committees. Interestingly, the two forms of organization – responsibility for EU affairs and the organization of support staff – do not always overlap, especially in the case of parliaments where sectoral committees play an important role in the scrutiny of EU affairs. The organization of EU staff is, however, important in that it has an impact on the extent to which sectoral committees receive advice on EU affairs and, by implication, on the effectiveness of these committees at scrutinizing EU dossiers.

The Dutch lower chamber is a case where the decision to put sectoral committees in charge of EU affairs in their policy areas went hand in hand with a corresponding administrative reform. The lower chamber has 10 EU staff, most of whom work for the sectoral committees. Each sectoral committee thus shares one specialist in EU affairs with one other committee. The EU specialists coordinate their activities horizontally once a week in a staff meeting. By contrast, in other parliaments where sectoral committees have EU responsibilities, either the 'normal' committee staff have to take on EU responsibilities (as in the Dutch second chamber) or the EAC staff or a central EU affairs staff advise the sectoral committees as required (as in the Belgian lower chamber).

In Sweden, where sectoral committees are responsible for document-based scrutiny and are comparatively well-staffed with about seven staff members per committee, the normal committee staff are expected to develop the necessary expertise (Hegeland 2015). Overall, despite the fact that sectoral committees play at least an advisory role in EU affairs in the majority of chambers, it also seems that the majority of sectoral committees do not have their own EU staff.

Instead, the most common form of EU support is through an EAC secretariat or a central EU unit. In fact, quite frequently the EAC secretariat is the only administrative EU unit, as is the case in, for example, France, Belgium, Hungary, Portugal and Slovenia. In other cases, they are complemented by a central unit responsible for inter-parliamentary relations or information management, as in the case of the Czech Republic, Germany, the Netherlands, Sweden, Croatia, Denmark and Luxembourg. In those cases where the central units are fairly large, as in the German Bundestag, they naturally have the capacity to allocate certain staff members to specific policy areas (Höing 2015). It is relatively rare for a parliament to have only a central unit and no specific committee staff at all, as in the Austrian and Greek cases. A number of parliaments also employ specialist legal staff or researchers – for example, those of Bulgaria, the Czech Republic, Estonia, Italy and Poland.

Finally, all but two parliaments (Slovakia and Bulgaria) currently have a representative in Brussels who maintains inter-parliamentary relations on a day-to-day basis, alerts the national parliament to new EU initiatives and facilitates contacts with the EU institutions (cf. Neuhold and Högenauer 2013). Some of the bicameral parliaments even have one representative per chamber. As was discussed in Chapter 3 in more detail, there are currently 32 NPRs in Brussels representing parliaments of 26 EU member states. These national parliamentary representatives have a potentially important role to play not only in terms of the vertical links they establish between Brussels and national legislatures, but also horizontally in facilitating coordination among parliaments in the EU (see also Chapter 3).

EU staff in perspective

Finally, it is also interesting to compare the role of officials working on EU affairs in the parliaments with the political advisors working in EU affairs – the assistants to MPs and party group staff – and the parliamentary staff working on domestic policies. A comparison with more overtly political staff is difficult due to the scarcity of data. However, it seems that there is just as much variation in the resources provided to political staff working on EU affairs as in the parliamentary administrations. In fact, their roles seem to vary even more across countries.

In essence, there are countries such as Germany where MPs and political parties have vast amounts of resources and can hire a number of staff. A German MP has about €15,800 per month at their disposal to hire staff for their constituency and Berlin offices (Deutscher Bundestag 2013). In addition, the parties are comparatively well-staffed. Thus, unlike most parliaments, Germany not only has one NPR per chamber in Brussels, but also its own liaison office where the parties are also represented. In Hungary it is estimated that 40–50 people work on EU affairs alongside the main administration, mainly as experts for the party groups (Ilonszki 2015). By contrast, Austrian, Dutch or Danish MPs cannot usually afford to hire academic staff of their own, but have to share an assistant between several MPs. Similarly, the Dutch parties have much more limited resources and employ hardly any EU staff (e.g. Interview 8). The Austrian parties can hire a certain number of staff financed by the parliament, which means they have at least one EU expert per group. These staff members work for MPs of both chambers. As a result, party staff members do the final check in the preselection process before the agendas go to the committees in Germany and Austria, but not in the Netherlands. Nonetheless, the choices of the parliamentary administration are rarely contested, because parliamentary administrations try to anticipate the preferences of MPs (Höing 2015; Miklin 2015). In Portugal, party staff or MPs usually draft the final documents for the EWS and thus limit the discretion of parliamentary administrations.

Parliamentary administrations tend to have some advantages over political staff. Thus, in several countries, parliamentary staff can take part in EU coordination meetings in the ministries and can gather first-hand information (Figulova 2015; Hrabálek and Strelkov 2015). They also, with the exception of the German political parties and their representatives in the Liaison Office, tend to be better connected to the EU level via the NPR, and tend to have better and more regular access to the information databases on EU affairs.

Another line of comparison is with parliamentary administrators in domestic affairs. Again, the overall impression is that EU staff members play a greater role in EU affairs than parliamentary administrations in domestic affairs. The only case in which the EU unit was perceived to be understaffed compared with the rest of the administration was Greece (Sotiropoulos 2015). In all other cases where such information was available, the EU units were either as well-staffed (cf. Hegeland

2015) or better staffed than comparable units responsible for domestic politics. For example, the EAC is one of the best staffed committees in Finland, with nine administrators compared with 3–9 for the other committees; in Hungary, eight staff compared with 2–3; and Luxembourg, with two administrators and one assistant compared with one administrator and one assistant at the most for other committees (cf. Spreitzer 2013; Ilonszki 2015; Raunio 2015). The Portuguese, Estonian and Danish EACs were seen to be somewhat better staffed (Christensen 2015; Ehin 2015; Jančić 2015).

This more generous allocation of resources in favour of EU affairs is, in part, recognition of the higher degree of complexity of EU issues and laws and, in part, also reflects the greater need for cooperation with other parliaments and EU institutions in this area. EU staff members also tend to hold some unique prerogatives compared with other parliamentary staff, especially when it comes to their agenda-setting powers as a result of the fact that they preselect relevant documents from among all incoming EU documents. Domestic legislation tends to require parliamentary action, which means that administrators do not have the discretion to sort legislative proposals into documents for consideration and documents that can be ignored. Overall, administrators dealing with EU affairs can be seen to be in a stronger position compared with both their colleagues responsible for domestic politics and the political staff in parliaments.

Conclusions

The discussion has provided a comparative perspective on the staff resources available to national parliaments and the organization of parliamentary administrators working on EU matters. In doing so, it has shed light on a rather underdeveloped area of parliamentary studies, falling as it were between the study of legislatures, focused on the work of MPs and political parties, and the study of administrations, focused on the executive. Parliaments have sizeable administrations, and delegate to these important tasks.

As we have seen, the extent of in-house expertise on EU affairs available to national parliaments varies considerably across member states. The number of EU experts employed by the individual chambers ranges from 1 to 44.5. This variation can be largely explained by the size of the chamber in terms of its number of MPs and by the size of its parliamentary administration more generally. However, it also seems to be the case that most chambers employ at least a certain 'critical minimum' number of staff – between four and five staff members. This is apparently the number of administrators that is generally regarded as necessary for the satisfactory completion of a certain number of basic support functions. Beyond that, the number of EU experts increases relatively slowly as the size of the overall parliamentary administration increases.

Interestingly, the staffing levels of national parliaments have developed differently over recent years. Whereas some parliaments employed more EU experts as the European competences of national parliaments expanded, other parliaments reduced the number of EU experts. The affected parliaments generally explained those reductions by reference to budgetary austerity and/or the Eurozone crisis. Thus, parliaments were exposed to two conflicting influences: strengthened powers through the Treaty of Lisbon, and budgetary pressures as a result of the Eurozone crisis – some parliaments reacted to one influence while others reacted to the alternative. On the whole, one can argue that the Eurozone crisis prevented the Lisbon Treaty from developing its full effect on the growth of parliamentary administrations.

In addition, through the analysis of the staff levels and the organization of EU experts in a comparative perspective, this chapter provides useful avenues for further analysis of the roles that the various parliamentary administrations can play in the scrutiny of EU affairs. Above all, the challenge remains to close the gap in the literature between legislatures and administrators, and thereby enable a more comprehensive understanding of the scrutiny of EU affairs at the national level. Chapter 5 will take up these issues by focusing on the tasks that are currently being delegated to parliamentary administrations and the implications of delegation on the bureaucratization of parliamentary scrutiny.

Interviews

Interview 1: Belgian Senate, EAC clerk, 16 April 2012.
Interview 2: Belgian House of Representatives, EAC clerk, 25 May 2012.
Interview 3: Dutch Tweede Kamer, Defence clerk, 27 March 2012.
Interview 4: Dutch Tweede Kamer, JHA clerk, 27 March 2012.
Interview 5: French Senate, advisor, 4 May 2012.
Interview 6: Romanian Senate, 2 clerks European Division, 12 April 2012.
Interview 7: Danish Folketing, EU advisors, 19 November 2012.
Interview 8: Tweede Kamer, MP VVD, 26 March 2012.
Written reply 1: EAC, Swedish parliament, 11 September 2012.
Written reply 2: EAC, French Senate, 19 November 2012.

Written reply 3: EAC, Finnish Eduskunta, 12 November 2012.
Written reply 4: EAC, UK House of Commons, 24 January 2013.
Written reply 5: EAC, Austrian Nationalrat and Bundesrat, 13 November 2012.
Written reply 6: EAC, Belgian Chamber of Deputies, 28 November 2012.
Written reply 7: EAC, German Bundestag, 5 December 2012.
Written reply 8: EAC, Luxembourg parliament, 30 November 2012.
Written reply 9: EAC, Belgian Senate, 22 November 2012.
Written reply 10: EAC, German Bundesrat, 6 December 2012.

5

The Europeanization of National Parliamentary Administrations: Convergence or Divergence?

Introduction

In light of the low participation in the elections to the European Parliament and the remaining limits on the powers of this institution, EU affairs scrutiny by national parliaments is increasingly regarded as an additional source of legitimacy for the EU. However, as national parliaments take centre stage in the debate about the need to enhance the democratic legitimacy of EU decision-making, it becomes ever more important to ask questions not only about the relationship between parliaments, on the one hand, and national governments and the EU institutions, on the other, but also to illuminate the internal processes within national parliaments and the horizontal networking among them.

Chapter 4 has shown that there are significant differences in the resources that national parliaments are able to devote to administrative support for the scrutiny of EU affairs, as well as considerable variations in the way national parliaments organize their procedures to facilitate this process. In other words, there appears to be considerable diversity among the legislatures of the EU member states, especially against the background of a trend towards greater mainstreaming of EU affairs within parliamentary chambers that leads some parliaments increasingly to involve sectoral committees in EU affairs scrutiny (Gattermann et al. 2013).

This chapter is, in part, based on A.L. Högenauer and C. Neuhold (2015), 'National Parliaments after Lisbon: Administrations on the Rise?', *West European Politics*, 38(2), 335–54, DOI: 10.1080/01402382.2014.990698

One key question is the extent to which administrators can facilitate the effective oversight of EU dossiers by individual chambers, or the creation of new bureaucratic networks that coordinate the information flow across parliaments (see: Chapter 3). A more influential role for administrators weighs on both sides of the 'scales of democratic legitimacy'. While, through their work, administrators have the capacity to facilitate the empowerment of national parliaments, this also raises new questions about shifting power from elected politicians to unelected officials. To the extent that the work of elected politicians depends on the input of unelected officials, electoral democracy risks being (partially) replaced by government through bureaucracy. As studies of executive bureaucracies point out, the power of bureaucrats vis-à-vis their 'political masters' at the head of ministries (cf. Hammond 1986; Egeberg 1995; Barberis 1996; Barker and Wilson 1997) – the Yes Minister syndrome – the same question could be asked in the context of legislatures: Are elected members in control of their agenda? Or is it possible that, under certain circumstances, civil servants working within parliamentary administrations 'call the shots' when it comes to parliamentary work?

So far, the focus on parliaments as political institutions has prevented the emergence of an academic debate about the roles of administrators in the scrutiny of EU affairs. However, the improved information rights of national parliaments increase the pressure on their procedures for information management, and the eight-week deadline to issue reasoned opinions under the EWS creates a further challenge. This chapter thus raises the question as to the extent to which parliamentary administrations play an active part in the scrutiny of EU politics, with a particular emphasis on the question related to the extent to which their tasks are purely 'technical' or have the potential to shape the actual outcome of parliamentary scrutiny. In the process, the chapter will try to address the question of whether the attempts to politicize and 'democratize' European policy-making by way of the Lisbon Treaty were, in fact, accompanied by a tendency towards bureaucratization, as argued by Christiansen et al. (2014). For this purpose, we attempt to classify and capture the tasks and roles of the various administrations with reference to the typology in Chapter 1 in order to be able to see the extent to which they are, in fact, merely technocratic (or not). In addition, this will allow us to understand the extent to which there is variation in the roles of the administrators of different parliaments.

For this purpose, the chapter will discuss the findings of the first comparative study of parliamentary administrations in European policy-making in the context of the ideal-typical roles that were set out in Chapter 1. It argues that parliamentary administrations play an active role in parliamentary scrutiny that goes beyond technical tasks and that can include even agenda-shaping. In conclusion, the extent of bureaucratization of parliamentary scrutiny of EU affairs is discussed.

The chapter focuses on parliamentary staff itself rather than the experts employed by party groups or those working for individual MPs. Whereas party group staff or personal assistants are meant to interpret policy issues according to a political stance, parliamentary administrators face the challenge of having to remain unbiased. The research was conducted in two stages: it comprises 39 semi-structured interviews with committee clerks and MPs from 11 member states between September 2010 and June 2013: the UK (House of Commons), France, Belgium, Germany (Bundesrat), the Netherlands, Sweden, Austria, Poland, Italy, Slovakia and Romania, as well as parliamentary representatives in Brussels from Slovenia, Finland and Ireland.[1] These cases cover a wide range of parliaments characterized by marked differences with regard to geographical location and the size of the respective parliament, and the activity of the legislature in EU affairs in general. In addition, the authors have received written replies to a questionnaire from 21 chambers that allow for a broader overview. By way of this data collection, 28 chambers in 21 member states are covered.[2]

Parliamentary administrations in EU affairs: Mere paper-pushers

To recapitulate briefly on Chapter 1, we argued that if we want to capture the differences between parliamentary administrations in a meaningful way, we need to develop a fine-tuned typology that distinguishes not just between tasks that are 'technical' and 'non-technical', but also between different shades of 'non-technical'. As many of the current challenges faced by national parliaments are related to information-processing, Chapter 1 thus proposed a typology that classified different aspects of information-processing on the basis of their potential for influence on the scrutiny process. In addition, national parliamentary administrations are conveniently located at one of the main sources of timely information, which greatly facilitates their exercise of information acquisition and management.

First, as seen in Chapter 3, the liaison officers of national parliaments in Brussels are a hub of information from other national parliaments and the EU institutions. A core task of these liaison officers is to ensure day-to-day coordination with other national parliaments, which is facilitated by the fact that the majority of these EU member states currently have such officers in Brussels, almost all of whom are located on the same floor of an EP building in Brussels. Thanks to their proximity to the European institutions, these officers also provide information to national parliaments about upcoming EU initiatives that could affect the country and parliament (cf. Neuhold and Högenauer 2013).

Second, in all parliaments, administrators are in charge of maintaining not only the collaborative databases on parliamentary opinions and reasoned opinions on EU policies, such as IPEX, but also the information system of their own parliament. They are thus the first 'recipients' of EU-related legislative documents and any accompanying documents from the government and EU institutions, and are the ones who 'feed' these documents into their own parliament's database and also, in some cases, to European affairs and/or sectoral committees.

Third, in some cases parliamentary administrators have access to the databases shared with the government, as in the case of the Czech Republic where, in practice, only the parliamentary administration – neither the MPs nor the political staff – take this opportunity (Hrabálek and Strelkov 2015). Finally, in a few cases, such as the Czech Republic and the Republic of Slovakia, they can attend coordination meetings in the ministries or, as is the case in Austria, with officials from ministries. Overall, this extensive access to information is important, as it is this information that allows national parliaments to formulate positions independent of government.

Hence, the typology (cf. Table 5.1) distinguished between five roles that largely evolve around information management: First, under an administrative analyst model, the administration would simply forward or summarize and forward information. Second, an analyst-type administration would offer legal and procedural advice and draft opinions on the basis of committee or plenary debates. Third, the administration could play an advisory role, which involves the provision of content-related advice and of drafts *prior* to debates. Fourth, an administration could play the role of agenda-shaper if it were tasked with the preselection of documents that are particularly relevant for parliament or specific committees. Finally, administrators can be involved in the coordination between national parliaments or between the chapters of a bicameral parliament. The first four roles are seen as incremental – that is, staff playing an advisory role may well also perform the tasks in the categories of analyst and assistant.

Table 5.1 Roles and tasks of parliamentary administrators in EU affairs

Roles	Administrative assistant	Analyst	Advisor	Agenda-shaper	Coordinator
Tasks	• Gathers and forwards information • Summarizes information • Organizes committee meetings	• Provides choice of balanced arguments* • Drafts after debates* • Procedural and legal advice	• Content-related advice • Drafts before debates*	• Preselection of documents	• Coordination with executive • Other parliaments • EU institutions • Internal coordination
Extent of involvement in scrutiny	Low	Low–medium	Medium	Medium–high	

Cf. Chapter 1.
*These nuanced distinctions were derived from the in-depth interview data.

A summary of the main results of our survey of national parliaments is presented in Table 5.2. The results will be discussed in greater depth below in connection with the interview data.

The background data reflects that the vast majority of administrations have a very extensive set of tasks and play an important supporting role in the scrutiny process. Moreover, we can also discern a general trend of officials providing both procedural guidance and advice as regards to content. It is noteworthy that this trend towards a certain degree of empowerment of officials not only prevails in member states that are seen as 'proactive and engaged' within EU decision-making, such as Denmark (O'Brennan and Raunio 2007: 21), but also in member states that have joined the European Union in the more recent rounds of enlargement. This is in line with the more general verdict that parliaments of the (relative) newcomers to the EU face shortcomings but that these are expected to diminish over time (Szalay 2005; Vehar 2007). There thus seems to be a trend towards convergence, leaving officials to play rather substantial roles in parliaments across the Union, at least when it comes to parliamentary scrutiny of EU affairs in the post-Lisbon EU.

Procedural advice and preselection

As Table 5.2 shows, the forwarding of information and the provision of procedural advice is one of the key responsibilities of the administrations of all chambers for which information is available. Thus, due to the

Table 5.2 Tasks of staff in EU affairs

		Tasks of EU staff			
		Selection documents	**Procedural advice**	**Drafting of the final position**	**Content advice**
Austria	Both chambers	Pre-check for subsidiarity	+	–	+
Belgium	Upper House	+	+	–	–
	Lower House	+	+	+	+
Bulgaria		+	+	+	+
Cyprus		+	+	–	+
Czech	Upper House	+	N.i.	N.i.	+
	Lower House	+	+	+	+
Denmark		+	+	–	+
Estonia		+	+	+	+
Finland		–	+	+	+
France	Upper House	+	+	+	+
	Lower House	+	+	N.i.	+
Germany	Upper House	+	+	–	+
	Lower House	+	+	+	–
Hungary		+	+	+	+
Italy	Lower House	+	+	+	+
Lithuania		N.i.	+	N.i.	+
Luxembourg		+	+	–	–
Netherlands	Upper House	–	+	+	On request
	Lower House	+	+	+	Yes, but balanced
Poland	Upper House	+	+	+	+
	Lower House	+	+	+	+
Portugal		–	+	Sometimes	+
Romania	Lower House	+	+	+	+
Slovakia		+	+	+	+
Sweden		+	+	Yes, but only on request	–
UK	Lower House	–	+	+	+

+ means that the administration perform this task; – means that it does not perform this task.
N.i. = no information.
Source: Questionnaires and interview data.

complex and legalistic nature of parliamentary involvement – especially under the EWS, all of the administrations play at least an important role as *analysts* who have to inform MPs of the options that are available to them.

In addition, the new rules on information provision led to national parliaments being swamped with information. Thus, national parliaments receive about 1,000 policy documents (e.g. legislative proposals) per year accompanied by about 24,000 supporting documents (e.g. EP opinions) per year (Höing 2015; Interview 1). As a result, all parliaments channel this information flow via their administration.

The European Affairs staff does not just act as a 'mailbox', but – in at least 21 cases – preselects documents based on their relevance for the member state and political salience, either based on the Commission Work Program, the weekly list of proposals or both (cf. Table 5.2). The extent to which administrations filter these documents varies across parliaments. In quantitative terms, the Belgian European Affairs clerk estimates that about 100–200 out of 1,000 documents – that is, 10–20 percent – are 'short-listed' for further scrutiny by parliamentary staff (Interview 1). The staff of the Belgian Senate recommends around 30–40 percent of documents to the committees for further scrutiny (Delreux and Randour 2015). The Dutch parliament selects only about 80 priority dossiers on an annual basis, based on the Commission work programme (Interview 2). Finally, the German Directorate PE Europe sends out information on around half of EU legislative drafts (Höing 2015).

These lists of priorities are, of course, of an advisory nature and usually subject to the approval of the European Affairs Committee, Specialized Committees or the Chair of the European Affairs Committee. Thus, in most cases, parliamentary administrations preselect the documents in accordance with the relevant committees, and administrators agree that their lists are generally accepted by their political masters (Interviews 2, 3, 4, 5, 6 and 7). The Sejm has, for example, never issued a reasoned opinion without an earlier suggestion from the Research Bureau (Interview 8). In practice, this filtering role thus provides parliamentary staff with an opportunity to act as *agenda-shapers*. In order to ensure that important dossiers are noticed, some parliamentary staff in addition provide specific procedural advice on how to follow the issue up (Interviews 9 and 10).

It should be noted that the role of the administration in preselection issues is specific to the EWS and document-based scrutiny. In the case of mandating, which is based on the agenda of the Council of Ministers and the draft position of the government on these issues, the tasks of the administration are based around the provision and analysis of preparatory information, rather than selection (Interviews 9 and 11). Nevertheless, in mandating systems the role of administrators is also strengthened insofar as there is now a clear list of priorities that the parliament will focus on and for which administrators can prepare.

Drafting and advice

As in the case of the filtering of documents, the practices on information-provision vary across chambers. Overall, at least 17 chambers allow their administrations to draft the final documents and 21 to provide content-related advice (cf. Table 5.2).

The interviews revealed more fine-tuned aspects of these variations. The administration of the Dutch Lower House, the Swedish parliament and the French parliament generally provide committees with balanced arguments on an issue. The administration of the Romanian House of Representatives provides an analysis only on request (Interviews 9, 12 and 13). The advantage of such a system is that administrators support the activities of MPs but, by providing them with a range of arguments and alternatives, they remain relatively neutral (cf. Meller 1952: 116). In the case of the Dutch Lower House, this provision of balanced arguments is part of an attempt to get politicians more actively involved in the scrutiny of EU affairs. Before the reform in 2006, the administrators often drafted the actual document before the debate, which could result in the committee simply approving a draft prepared beforehand. As the committees are now confronted with potentially contradictory arguments, they have at the very least to choose from among the list of arguments (Interview 9).

Those administrations that only provide summaries of documents or a list of different arguments usually also only draft parliamentary documents *after* the debates in the committees. The EAC staff of the German Bundesrat, for example, drafts reasoned opinions based on the debates in the Bundesrat (Interview 14).

In rare cases, parliamentary administrations already provide drafts *prior* to debates in the committee – for example, the European Affairs clerks of the Belgian House of Representatives, the Romanian Senate and the Polish Sejm (Interviews 1, 15 and 16), as well as the French parliamentary administration for reasoned opinions (Interview 13) or the Slovak parliament on request of the chair (Interview 17). In the Romanian case, the lack of interest on the part of politicians can often either render administrative preparatory work redundant due to lack of political activity or lead to a simple rubber-stamping of drafts provided by staff (cf. Strelkov 2015).

The duties of parliamentary staff with regard to mandating are similar to those under parliamentary scrutiny in this regard. Administrators gather information on the Council meeting and government position, and advise the relevant committee (Interview 11). In the case of the Dutch parliament – and sometimes also the Polish Senate – the administration sometimes even drafts possible questions to the minister (Interviews 9 and 18).

A coordination function

In addition to the tasks outlined above and in Table 5.2, parliamentary administrations play an important coordinating function across national parliaments. A central element of that are, of course, the coordination between national parliaments and the coordination between national parliaments and the European institutions, which are primarily assured by the liaison officers in Brussels. The role of these officers has been discussed extensively in Chapter 3.

However, in addition to the liaison officers in Brussels, the EU experts in national parliaments assume some coordination functions. Traditionally, they do not have many direct contacts in other national parliaments and only some contacts in EU institutions. The main responsibility of the committee staff and central staff units of national parliaments is to assure the coordination and communication with national ministries (e.g. Interviews 3, 9, 19 and 20). This means that, de facto, most inter-parliamentary cooperation and requests for information run via the network of liaison officers in Brussels.

However, as the EWS encourages inter-parliamentary cooperation, parliamentary staff have started to see the advantage of an enhanced network of the main staff of parliaments. As a result, due to a Dutch initiative, a meeting of the clerks of European Affairs Committees took place after the COSAC meeting of April 2012 (Interview 21). It was the first meeting in many years and was motivated by the increased need for coordination (Interview 6).

In addition, parliamentary staff can also play a role in the coordination between the two chambers of bicameral parliaments. In the Netherlands, for example, cooperation between the two chambers is ensured mainly via administrative cooperation. Thus, the EU staff of the Senate takes part regularly in the Tuesday morning meetings of the EU staff of the Lower House. Even when the two chambers issue joint reasoned opinions, the coordination takes place mostly via the administration. However, this close cooperation is specific to the Netherlands. Neither the French nor the Belgian chambers work so closely together and, thus, neither do their administrations (Interviews 9, 20, 22 and 23).

Finally, parliamentary clerks play a role in *intraparliamentary* cooperation. The Dutch EU advisors of all standing committees coordinate horizontally which committees should best discuss a certain issue. If several committees are involved, they facilitate the communication between those fora. In Denmark, where sectoral committees are consulted before the EAC mandates the government, the EU and committee staff are also responsible for compiling the different views and ensuring that the various parliamentary actors are aware of their activities (Interviews 24 and 25). Naturally, the multiple memberships in committees mean that there is usually also at least one MP on the EAC who also sits on the relevant sectoral committee. In addition, committee staff also act as institutional memory, as some EU legislative processes span several years (Interview 26).

Summary

Overall, the empirical analysis of the tasks of the EU staff of national parliaments confirms the criticism of existing typologies of staff roles. First, the parliamentary administrations of all 28 chambers were *all* found to perform at least some functions that go beyond the merely technical. Second, the differences between parliamentary administrations are fairly nuanced and thus require a nuanced typology.

Interestingly, empirically *none* of the parliamentary administrations falls exclusively into the category of administrative assistant. All parliaments rely on their administrations for additional non-technical support and thus allow their administrators to play some role in the scrutiny of EU affairs. In addition, only the administration of the Dutch Upper House was limited to the role of analyst, by way of giving procedural advice, for example. Five parliamentary administrations also provided content-related advice and/or drafts prior to debates and thus act as *advisors*. The vast majority of administrations, however, falls into the category of *agenda-shaper*: 21 chambers allowed their administrations to preselect documents for parliamentary scrutiny. Finally, administrators can fulfil a coordinating function vis-à-vis other national parliaments, European institutions or their own government.

Table 5.3 reflects the relative homogeneity of tasks that officials perform across parliaments.

Overall, the preparation for and implementation of the Treaty of Lisbon has allowed administrators to play a more active role in EU affairs. Administrators have become active advisors and even 'steer' parliamentary business to some extent. Despite the fact that national parliaments are often seen to invest less energy in European issues rather

Table 5.3 Roles of parliamentary administrations (2013)*

Administrative assistant	Analyst	Advisor	Agenda-shaper
	Dutch Upper House	Austria (both)**, Finland, Portugal, UK (Lower House) (Lithuania?)***	Belgium (both), Bulgaria, Cyprus, Czech (both), Denmark, Estonia, France (both), Germany (both), Hungary, Italian Lower House, Luxembourg, Dutch Lower House, Poland (both), Romanian Lower House, Slovakia, Sweden

Note: *The coordination function is not listed here; all parliamentary administrations play this role. Variation exists only as to the range of coordination tasks.
**The Austrian parliament has an administrative unit that conducts a 'pre-check' for subsidiarity concerns. However, its activities are narrowly circumscribed (e.g. through politically defined key words), which makes it a border line case between preselection and advice. As the drafting function of the EU staff is also limited, we count it as a strong advisor.
***The Lithuanian parliament is at least an advisor. However, as information is missing on preselection, for example, it cannot be assessed whether it is also an agenda-shaper.

than in domestic issues, the EU units are comparatively well-staffed (e.g. in terms of EAC staff compared with sectoral committee staff) (Högenauer and Christiansen 2015). Moreover, EU staff can have more powers than domestic staff, the preselection role being a case in point (Spreitzer 2013). Both of these features are, of course, in line with delegation theory, which suggests that delegation is more likely on complex issues and on issues that are perceived as being less salient.

However, the question is also whether this bureaucratization is necessarily problematic from a normative point of view, which would only be the case if officials would evade the instructions of their political principals. So far, this does not appear to be the case as most interviewees agree, for instance, that the preselection of documents by administrators is rarely contested.

While most parliamentary administrations perform similar roles to begin with, the remaining variation between parliaments is difficult to explain conclusively on the basis of this first comparative data collection on parliamentary administrations and in the absence of prior studies. There are, however, some patterns that one might logically expect.

One hypothesis would be that the size and tasks of parliamentary administrations might depend on the size of the parliament. Smaller parliaments or parliaments from economically weaker member states may not have the resources for a large bureaucratic apparatus, which would limit the amount of support that the administration could provide.

Alternatively, one might expect mandating systems giving rise to more political contestation as they touch on the relationship between opposition parties, the executive and parties in government. Delegation to the administration can be expected to be more limited, as political actors would be expected to want to stay in control of issues that are attributed political importance (Wlezien 2005).

Lastly, one might expect a link between pro-active and engaged parliaments (O'Brennan and Raunio 2007) and strong administrations, although with a different causal direction: a strong administration might *enable* a parliament to engage actively and effectively in parliamentary scrutiny.

However, even a cursory comparison of the data in Table 5.3 with data on the ratio between staff numbers and MPs (Högenauer and Christiansen 2015), the level of activity of parliaments (Auel et al. 2015b) or the existing mandating systems shows that the most extensive type of role is performed both by cases that are, in fact, in line with the hypotheses *and* by cases that clearly contradict them (e.g. Estonia, Slovakia, Belgium and Cyprus). Similarly, the group of somewhat weaker administrations also contains very different cases (e.g. the British House of Commons shares few characteristics with the Dutch Upper House).

The fact that many of the 'obvious' variables, such as resources, do not have a clear relationship with the typology of the roles of administration suggests that there may be deeper reasons for the variation. This could be less about constraints and opportunities but, rather, about *choice and administrative traditions*. What *is* an appropriate role for a parliamentary administration? What *should* it do? It is possible that there is a gap between parliaments that emphasize *efficiency* (i.e. the administration carries the main burden) and parliaments that emphasize *political* control (i.e. certain tasks should fall within the scope of political masters). Our interviews reflect that the decision of the Dutch Tweede Kamer only to provide balanced arguments – rather than concrete recommendations – is rooted in the desire to stimulate political debate (Interview 9). However, to assess these logics of appropriateness across a wider range of cases would require further in-depth studies. Ideally, in order to provide further explanation, the comparison should focus on the variance between parliamentary administrations that perform a comprehensive range of tasks and administrations whose tasks are limited in the context of parliaments that are otherwise very similar (when it comes to size and system of scrutiny for example).

Subtle variation: The case of the German Bundestag, the Dutch Lower House, the Danish Folketing and the Austrian parliament

Our data reflects that even a fine-tuned scale of administrative roles brings, at first sight, only limited variation between national parliaments to the fore. Most parliaments appear to belong to the same category and delegate extensively to their administrations. Nevertheless, this apparent uniformity is deceptive. There are differences even between strong administrations – both in their organization and in the performance of their functions. This has to do both with how EU affairs scrutiny has developed historically, and with the resources available to MPs more generally. In order to illustrate this diversity, this section will look briefly at four parliaments that have been relatively active in EU affairs scrutiny and that delegate rather extensive tasks to their administrations.

The German Bundestag

The German Lower House, the Bundestag, has one of the largest EU affairs administrations among national parliaments (Schäfer 2013). Around 2,800 employees work for the Bundestag (Linn and Sobolewski 2012), and it employed around 45 staff members for EU affairs in the period 2011–13. With this level of staff, the Bundestag delegates extensively to its administration. However, the Bundestag has also exceptionally well-staffed party groups, so that 'politicized administrators' – party group staff – can counterbalance and control the core administration of the parliament. The influence of party group staff is felt early on. Whereas most national parliaments have only one representative in Brussels or, at best one, for each parliamentary chamber, the German Bundestag is represented both by the main administration and, since early 2007, also by representatives of the political parties. The Bundestag thus not only receives information on forthcoming EU proposals from representatives of its central administrative unit for EU affairs, the Directorate PE Europe, but each party group receives reports from its own staff (Höing 2015).

Inside the Bundestag, the EU affairs administration is centralized in the PE Europe Directorate and the EAC secretariat. However the generous staffing levels of these units allow for a certain amount of specialization in EU affairs. Thus, the PE Europe Directorate was subdivided into four departments in 2013. Each department deals with a certain policy remit. One of them is, for example, responsible for following up on the new intergovernmental treaties regarding the Eurozone crisis and the EU's budgetary rules. The sectoral committees of the Bundestag, which play an active role in EU affairs scrutiny, receive their information directly from these central units (Höing 2015).

In everyday work, the juxtaposition of party staff and core administration continues. The PE Europe Directorate plays an agenda-setting role, in that it draws up priority lists of incoming documents related to EU affairs and makes recommendations as to the committees that should follow each issue. The staff of the European Affairs Committee mainly organizes the work of the EAC, but also provides advice to other committees on request (Höing 2015). The priority lists of the parliamentary administration are checked by party group staff, who can change them (Winzen 2014). However, Höing estimates that around 95 percent of the proposals are accepted (2015). By the time these lists reach the EU coordinators of the party groups, they are almost complete and only a few questions remain to be discussed (Winzen 2014).

The Danish Folketing

The Danish Folketing is another active player in EU affairs. It benefits from strong mandating powers in combination with weak minority governments that need to create majorities for every issue. However, unlike the Bundestag, where sectoral committees are expected to take the initiative on EU policy issues falling into their domains, the Danish mandating system in EU affairs has concentrated the power in the hands of the EAC. As a result, the administration of EU affairs in the Folketing is also highly centralized. Staff resources are therefore concentrated on the EAC.

The EAC of the Folketing currently comprises three EU consultants, two committee clerks and five assistants. As in the German case, this level of staffing still allows for some specialization. One advisor looks at issues related to the Common Agricultural Policy, for example, and one at issues related to the financial crisis. However, a high level of specialization is not possible and everybody has to be able to deal with all issues. In the end, the EU staff comprises 'specialists in procedures more than substance' (Interview 6).

While the EU staff of the Folketing is similarly centralized as the staff of the Bundestag, its tasks differ somewhat from those of their German colleagues. They also preselect incoming documents and thus perform an agenda-setting role but, apart from that, greater priority is given to the provision of content-related advice. In addition, the staff is not systematically involved in the drafting of opinions and reasoned opinions. Ideally, these documents should be drafted by party staff or the spokespersons of the majority on the basis of the discussion in the committees. Also, the parties that are in a minority are expected to provide minority statements, if they want these to be included. Drafting is thus done by a mix of administrative and political actors (Interviews 6, 24 and 27).

Finally, an important difference between the Folketing and the Bundesrat is the role of party staff. Unlike in the Bundestag, the staff resources of parties and individual MPs are very limited in the case of Denmark. The Socialist People's Party, for example, has only one EU expert. She plays an important role in the coordination of the party's contacts with MEPs and the coordination of the party's position on EU issues. However, in terms of information management, the main administration is seen as being of prime importance (Interview 28). As a result, the Folketing – like almost all parliaments – has only one representative in Brussels, who is a member of the European affairs administration of the parliament. As a result, the main administration has an information advantage over the political parties, and the preselection of documents is virtually exclusively in the hands of that administration.

Another important feature of the administration of the Folketing is the existence of an EU information centre with four academic staff. The mission of this centre is the provision of 'neutral' information to both politicians and the general public (Christensen 2015). This office is rooted in the EU-critical atmosphere of Danish politics. It was created in 1993 because of the debates about the ratification of the Treaty of Maastricht; these debates created a demand for information that did not come from the European Parliament or the Commission (who normally run these offices) (Interview 6). 'Neutral' or 'non-biased' are thus terms not so much about party politics or a government-parliament divide, but simply refer to a non-EU perspective.

The Dutch Tweede Kamer

The Dutch Lower House, the Tweede Kamer, is another fairly active parliament that has undertaken several reforms since the early 2000s to optimize its procedures for EU affairs scrutiny. One result of these reforms has been a complete mainstreaming of EU affairs scrutiny: in other words, each sectoral committee is fully responsible for the scrutiny of EU issues that fall into its area of specialization (Högenauer 2015). As a result of these reforms, the organization of the EU staff of the Tweede Kamer is radically different from that of the Bundestag or the Folketing.

Unlike its Danish and German counterparts, the Tweede Kamer has a relatively small central unit in the form of the secretariat of the European Affairs Committee. The EAC staff comprises only the actual committee advisors and the coordinator of all EU staff of the Tweede Kamer. Most of the EU experts are allocated to sectoral committees. Thus, normally about two committees share one EU advisor who deals *only* with EU issues, and not with other committee business, but who is formally embedded in the staff of those committees. In total, there are nine full-time experts and the coordinator, who ensures the horizontal coordination of EU affairs at the administrative level (Tweede Kamer 2011). The EU staff of the Tweede Kamer meets every Tuesday to coordinate the EU activities and debates in the House. Both EAC staff and the staff of sectoral committees are in regular contact with the relevant staff in the other chamber to alert each other to potentially problematic documents and to assist the chambers in adopting joint opinions in the event of similar views (Interviews 9 and 20).

The staff of the Tweede Kamer performs the full range of tasks, from the preselection of documents, via procedural advice, to the provision of content-related advice and the drafting of opinions and reasoned opinions after the debates in the committees. The EU staff of the sectoral committees is involved in both preselection of potential priorities from the Commission Work Programme, and preselection of incoming documents every week (Interview 29). What is specific to the staff of the Tweede Kamer is that they have tried to stimulate political debate by providing advice in a balanced pro/contra style. This approach encourages politicians to reflect critically on policy issues and potential arguments before voting on an issue (Interview 9).

While Dutch parties have some staff at their disposal, the main administration of the Tweede Kamer is not controlled by party staff, as such. Some parties, such as D66 and CDA have their own experts in EU affairs. These parties benefit from an independent source of information. However, as in the Danish case, an important part of the work of group staff is to provide coordination inside the party and to assist with the political interpretation of the facts (Interview 30). Thus, the main check on the EU staff of the parliament comprises the committee chairs and committee members in their daily work.

The Austrian parliament

The Austrian parliament is another rather strong player in EU affairs, at least on paper. This is due its mandating system (Blümel and Neuhold 2001).[3] Article 23(e) and Article 23k(3) of the Austrian Constitution stipulate that the EACs of the Nationalrat (lower house) can formulate opinions that legally bind the government in all negotiations on EU projects that need to be implemented into Austrian federal law. The government can deviate from these opinions only for 'urgent reasons of foreign or integration policy' and only after consulting the EAC once more. If constitutional law is affected, it may do so only if the EAC – after being consulted for a second time – does not raise an objection within the given time limit. The Bundesrat (upper house) has similar rights, but only with regard to measures that would restrict its own competencies or when constitutional law is affected (Miklin 2015).

It is noteworthy that Austria anticipated the Constitutional Treaty and its possible impact on the national legislature. Thus, in 2006, a special unit was created up within the 'EU and International Services' of the Parliamentary Directorate (*Parlamentsdirektion*). This unit was to deal with the increased information influx resulting from an enhanced role for national parliaments foreseen in the new treaty. In the practical political process, two divisions thus currently assist parliament with its EU-related tasks: the EU Coordination unit and the European Relations unit. Note that these units support both parliamentary chambers. All EU draft legislation is submitted to a pre-subsidiarity check here according to legal criteria. Draft legislation is thus prepared in such a way that it is given certain code words on a weekly basis. MPs making up the EACs of both chambers then receive recommendations by email (3–4 per week) on the type of issues on which a subsidiarity check could be performed.

The list containing the preselection of subsidiarity checks (*Vorpruefungsliste*) is not politically binding but simply a formal evaluation of dossiers that might, legally speaking, transgress the subsidiarity principle (Miklin 2015). The advisors of the political parties represented in the Austrian parliament scrutinize this list for political relevance.[4] In selected cases, this is coordinated with officials and members of Parliament of the respective sectoral committees on a case-by-case basis.

Sectoral committees are, however, so far not formally involved in Austrian EU affairs scrutiny. Once the list has been compiled, positions are coordinated *across* political cleavages. This is done via a weekly *jour fixe*, where all the political group advisors and officials working within the Parliamentary Directorate agree to what will be on the agenda of the EACs of the Nationalrat or the Bundesrat.[5] Usually, the wishes of the political groups are respected and the agenda of the respective EACs is agreed on consensually.

The decision to issue a reasoned opinion is determined by political objectives and opinions. The agenda is also determined by the availability of the respective ministers that have to attend the respective meeting of the EAC of the Nationalrat.[6] For the practical process, this might imply that a meeting might be scheduled with some delay (between the *jour fixe* and the actual meeting) depending on the (full) agenda of ministers.

Once agreement has been reached to draw up a reasoned opinion, it is normally the political group advisors that come up with a draft. In some cases, MPs also come up with the draft for the reasoned opinion themselves or negotiate amendments into the proposed reasoned opinion. The reasoned opinion itself is typically adopted in the EU Subcommittee of the Nationalrat or by the EAC of the Bundesrat (depending on which chamber is adopting the reasoned opinion) (Mastenbroek et al. 2014).

Conclusion

The Treaty of Lisbon has created new opportunities not only for national parliaments, but also for their administrations. In particular, the work-intensive system of document-based scrutiny under the new EWS has led to the delegation of certain tasks to administrators – for example, the filtering and preselection of relevant documents. The majority of parliamentary administrations do have the opportunity to shape the agenda of their respective legislature, at least to some extent. This can be further explained by the very nature of parliamentary scrutiny of EU affairs, as these issues are predominantly complex and touch on issues of low salience (Manley 1968).

In addition, EU staff plays an important role in the coordination between national parliaments. The permanent representatives of the respective national parliaments in the European Parliament (or, as they are called in the practical political process, 'liaison officers') are best placed to engage in information exchange on a regular basis and alert other parliaments to important proposals coming out of the EU's machinery (see Chapter 3).

The extent of delegation raises the question as to whether bureaucratic activity is *facilitating* political control or *replacing* it. However, while parliamentary administrations play a crucial role in parliamentary scrutiny, this bureaucratization does not necessarily present a threat to political control. According to our observations thus far, final decisions are taken by MPs in the (European Affairs or sectoral) committees and plenary and, so far, the coordination between MPs and administrations is by and large devoid of conflict. As a result, parliamentary administrations can, indeed, be seen as a pillar of support in the context of national parliamentary control of EU policy-making. The greatest impact of administrators on the scrutiny of EU affairs stems ultimately from their attempts to promote the discussion of important European issues within their parliaments.

Nevertheless, this first comparative study of the role of parliamentary administrations in EU affairs scrutiny ends in a puzzle. There is relatively little cross-national variation, but the variation that exists – which became obvious by way of the four cases presented in this chapter – does not follow any obvious pattern. One of the tasks for future research will thus be to explore further the differences between national systems of parliamentary administrative support, as well as the factors explaining the variation in administrative organization and tasks.

Interviews

Interview 1: Belgian House of Representatives, EAC clerk, 25 May 2012.
Interview 2: Dutch parliament, NPR, 9 December 2010.
Interview 3: House of Commons, EAC clerk, 23 May 2012.
Interview 4: French Senate, advisor, 4 May 2012.
Interview 5: Italian House of Representatives, EAC clerk, 9 November 2012.
Interview 6: Danish parliament, EU advisor, 19 November 2012.
Interview 7: Austrian parliament, NPR, 22 November 2010.
Interview 8: Polish Sejm, Research Bureau, 19 April 2013.
Interview 9: Dutch Lower House, EU Affairs clerk, 09 December 2011.
Interview 10: Romanian parliament, Former EU Staff, 17 November 2011.
Interview 11: Swedish parliament, EAC clerk, 13 March 2012.
Interview 12: Swedish parliament, Social Insurance Committee clerks, 6 March 2012.

Interview 13: French Senate, senior EU clerk (1), 25 May 2012.
Interview 14: German Bundesrat, EAC clerk, 4 May 2012.
Interview 15: Romanian Senate, EAC clerk, 5 April 2012.
Interview 16: Polish Sejm, EAC clerk, 23 April 2013.
Interview 17: Slovak parliament, EAC clerk, 29 May 2013.
Interview 18: Polish Senate, EAC advisor, 10 April 2013.
Interview 19: French Senate, EAC clerk, 12 May 2012.
Interview 20: Dutch Senate, 2 EAC clerks, 11 January 2012.
Interview 21: COSAC, 24 May 2012.
Interview 22: Belgian Senate, EAC clerk, 16 April 2012.
Interview 23: French Senate, EAC clerk (2), 25 May 2012
Interview 24: Danish parliament, Environment Clerk, 20 November 2012.
Interview 25: Danish parliament, Food, Agriculture and Fisheries Clerk, 27 November 2012.
Interview 26: Danish Parliament, EAC clerk, 21 November 2012.
Interview 27: Danish Parliament, Foreign Policy Clerk, 20 November 2012.
Interview 28: Danish Parliament, MP from the SSP, 27 November 12.
Interview 29: Dutch Lower House, two EU experts, 27 March 12.
Interview 30: Dutch Lower House, EAC clerk, 28 March 12.

6

New Tasks, Limited Resources: Regional Parliamentary Administrations in EU Affairs

Introduction

A combination of revisions of European Treaties and national constitutional reforms have – as a general rule – led to a strengthening of parliaments in the EU since the Single European Act (Hrbek 2010). However, initially, treaty reforms primarily benefited the EP, whereas national reforms and more recent treaty reforms have also considered the role of national parliaments. European integration has thus been a particularly great challenge for regional parliaments. Regions are less well-represented in EU policy-making than member states. In addition, the dominant actors in regional interest representation, both in intra-state coordination and in Brussels, are *regional governments*. As a result, until the Treaty of Lisbon, the role of regional parliaments in EU policy-making was mainly limited to controlling their regional executives, which were themselves often playing a subordinated role in the EU policy processes.

However, this should not disguise the fact that there are currently eight member states in the EU where regional parliaments have legislative powers in domestic policy-making: Austria, Belgium, Germany, the UK, Spain, Italy, Portugal and Finland. For these parliaments, European integration brought the same risks of disempowerment that are commonly observed at the national level. As with national parliaments, regional parliaments have, in the past, tended to be reactive institutions vis-à-vis their executives (Raunio and Wright 2006: 281–82). In addition, the informational imbalance between executives and legislatures in the EU decision-making system presents a challenge to accountability (O'Brennan and Raunio 2007: 4; Rittberger 2010: 240; Benz 2011: 1).

As a result, authors have voiced concerns that the legislative and control functions of regional parliaments and their ability to shape policy content constructively might become impaired as a result of integration (Abels and Eppler 2011: 20–21; Sprungk 2011: 213). Thus, it is estimated that 85–90 percent of all legislation that was passed at the national level in Austria in 2005 and 75 percent of all legislation in Germany was influenced by EU policy (Bußjäger 2010: 106; Sturm and Zimmermann-Steinhart 2005: 53, cited in Bußjäger 2010: 106). It should be noted that 'influenced' in this context does not mean that domestic legislation merely transposed European integration; it can also mean that the margin of manoeuvre of the legislators was limited by pre-existing European rules.

Yet, as in the case of national parliaments, the Treaty of Lisbon appears to have given new impetus to the European affairs scrutiny of regional parliaments, even if regional parliaments have been slower to react than national parliaments. Whereas many national parliaments anticipated likely constitutional changes at the European level after the failed Constitutional Treaty (e.g. the Dutch Tweede Kamer in 2006), reforms on the regional level have, as a general rule, taken place much later than at the national level – usually *after* the Lisbon Treaty came into force, and often only in 2012/2013. Scepticism also remains with regard to the ability of regional parliaments to make full use of the new opportunities and to control their own governments (cf. Vara Arribas and Högenauer 2015). Regional parliaments tend to be much smaller than their national counterparts and thus face considerably more severe limitations when it comes to resources. As this chapter shows, both the number of staff and the number of politicians working on EU affairs are much smaller compared with national parliaments. Nevertheless, the spreading reforms and the revival of inter-parliamentary cooperation at the regional level (Hrbek 2010; Eppler 2014; Vara Arribas and Högenauer 2015) show that regional parliaments try to strengthen their role in EU policy-making.

Overall, regional parliaments face at least two challenges that raise questions about their administrations: the information gap compared with regional and national governments, who have better access to Council documents, and their generally smaller size compared with national parliaments. Thus, this chapter seeks to understand how regional parliamentary administrations compare with national parliamentary administrations and, in particular, the extent to which they can reduce the 'information gap' while facing severe resource constraints. For this purpose, we will first discuss the new opportunities for regional parliaments after Lisbon. The second section provides an overview of the general resources of regional parliaments and the tasks of parliamentary administrations, and allows for a direct comparison with the national level. The tasks of administrators will thus be compared with the typology developed in Chapter 1. The third section will further elaborate on this through a qualitative analysis of three Belgian sub-national parliaments, which also draws parallels to the Scottish Parliament and the (limited) existing literature on the German Länder.

Regional parliaments after Lisbon: New powers – New impetus

In the 'Protocol on the Application of the Principles of Subsidiarity and Proportionality' of the Lisbon Treaty, sub-national parliaments are, for the first time, formally mentioned in EU primary law. In Article 4, the Treaty on European Union (TEU) recognizes the principle of regional and local autonomy. The principle of subsidiarity is further strengthened in Article 5 TEU and by the fact that the Committee of the Regions has gained the right to appeal to the European Court of Justice (ECJ) for the annulment of an act on the grounds of subsidiarity.

Most importantly for regional parliaments with legislative powers, they are to be consulted under the EWS. The detailed procedure of the EWS in the context of national parliaments has been discussed in previous chapters but, in essence, the Protocol states that national parliaments are to receive all legislative proposals, that they have eight weeks to assess a proposal after it has been published in all official languages and that they can object to the proposal on grounds of subsidiarity in a so-called 'reasoned opinion' within the limits of that deadline (cf. Introduction to this volume). However, the reasoned opinions are non-binding, and even if enough reasoned opinions are received to issue a so-called 'yellow card' or 'orange card', the EU institutions are not obliged to withdraw or amend the legislative proposal. With regard to regional parliaments, Article 6 of the Protocol, states that:

> it will be for each national Parliament or each chamber of a national Parliament to consult, where appropriate, regional parliaments with legislative powers.
>
> (Art. 6, Protocol 2, TFEU)

For regional parliaments, this presents a new opportunity for participation in EU policy-making via their national parliaments. However, the precise terms of participation are not defined but are left to be negotiated at the national level. In those member states where legislative regions exist, national parliaments have, in general, agreed to consult the regional parliaments with legislative powers, but the procedures vary substantially. For example, some national parliaments include a summary (i.e. their interpretation) of the position of regional parliaments in their own reasoned opinion, whereas others, such as the Belgian parliament, simply forward a regional reasoned opinion in its original form (cf. Vara Arribas and Högenauer 2015). As their arguments are forwarded in their original wording, Belgian regions are thus in a relatively advantageous position.

However, in general the fact that national parliaments have to meet an eight-week deadline means that regional parliaments have to meet a six- to seven-week deadline if they want their national parliament to be able to take their views into account. After all, the national parliament has to meet a strict eight-week deadline if it wants its vote(s) to count. Thus, the time pressure on regional parliaments is even greater than that on national parliaments and represents a substantial challenge to scrutiny. For example, the Scottish parliament was unable to provide the House of Commons and House of Lords with reasoned opinions in time during the first years of the EWS. Despite the fact that it had prepared for the introduction of the EWS by participating in the pilot studies of COSAC on subsidiarity alongside national parliaments, its procedures could not cope with the short deadlines (Raunio and Wright 2006: 293; Vara Arribas and Bourdin 2011: 122; Högenauer 2016). One has to take into account the fact that the EACs of regional parliaments are often also responsible for other issues (e.g. international affairs in the Scottish case) and often do not meet on a weekly basis. The meetings of the Scottish EAC are fairly irregular. It sometimes meets every week, as in May 2014, but then it sometimes takes breaks of three or more weeks – for example, in September and October 2014. Thus, one of the obstacles that prevented the Scottish parliament initially from adopting reasoned opinions was that, depending on the timing of the Commission proposal, it could be quite difficult to identify the proposal as potentially problematic, analyse it, discuss it, draft a reasoned opinion and have the plenary vote on that all within six to seven weeks.

Based on Fleischer's analysis of the database of regional parliaments and governments on subsidiarity (REGPEX, extranet.cor.europa.eu/subsidiarity/regpex/Pages/default.aspx), where regional parliaments and governments can exchange their views on subsidiarity, only 34 reasoned opinions (EWS) and 53 opinions (political dialogue) were recorded by regional parliaments between 2008 and 2013. According to Fleischer, this data underestimate the real number of opinions, as regional parliaments do not always upload their documents (Fleischer 2014). However, the numbers illustrate that regional output is relatively weak, if we take into account that this level of activity has been produced by 75 regional parliaments. By comparison, the national parliaments submitted 2,431 opinions under the political dialogue and 319 reasoned opinions between 2008 and 2013.

However, regional parliaments have also become considerably more active in inter-parliamentary cooperation since the mid-2000s, which has resulted in the establishment and/or increased use of mechanisms of cooperation (cf. Figure 6.1). In part, this is facilitated by the new focus of the Committee of the Regions on subsidiarity. As the Committee of the Regions obtained the right to appeal to the ECJ on grounds of subsidiarity, it embraced its role of guardian of subsidiarity and actively worked with regional actors on these issues (Domorenok 2009: 160).

Despite the fact that parliaments with legislative powers are in a clear minority in the Committee of the Regions, it has developed tools similar to the IPEX system used by national parliaments – for example, REGPEX. The REGPEX database is connected to the EU legislative databases OEIL and PreLex and allows its members to check the current

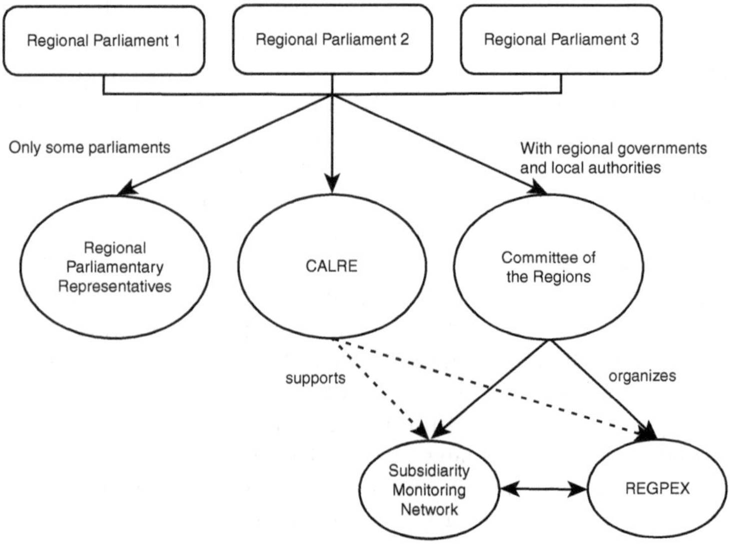

Figure 6.1 Inter-parliamentary cooperation of regional parliaments
Source: Author.

status of legislation as well as to upload their own opinions (Stahl 2009: 139–40). Of the regional parliaments, 43 are members of REGPEX, which means that more than half of all regional parliaments with legislative powers participate in it (Vara Arribas and Högenauer 2015). In 2005, the Committee of the Regions created the Subsidiarity Monitoring Network (SMN), which conducted subsidiarity tests, similar to those conducted by COSAC. These tests have helped regional parliaments to build expertise and develop their procedures for EU affairs scrutiny. In June 2013, the SMN had 146 partners including regional parliaments and governments, as well as local authorities and associations.

In addition, the Conference of Legislative Assemblies of Regions, CALRE, representing 74 regions from all eight member states, has become more active again in recent times. It brings together the presidents of the parliaments and currently focuses on the subsidiarity principle and inter-parliamentary cooperation. It discusses, for example, participation in the political dialogue with the European Commission and cooperation with the SMN of the Committee of the Regions (CALRE 2011).

Finally, some regional parliaments are now sending administrators to Brussels as parliamentary representatives. They try to emulate the work and functions of the network of national parliamentary representatives in the EP (cf. Chapter 3), although so far only a few regional parliaments have the resources to have a permanent official in Brussels.

The EU staff of regional parliaments

The data on regional parliaments with legislative powers was gathered in a similar manner to that on national parliaments. On the one hand, a written questionnaire was sent to the parliamentary administrations with questions about resources, organization and core tasks. Out of 75 regional parliaments with legislative powers, 21 replied to the questionnaire, which corresponds to a response rate of 28 percent. The low response rate is not particularly unusual, given the limited staff or regional parliaments. In addition, as regional parliaments are traditionally less international in their focus compared with national parliaments, the language barriers are also greater. The data nevertheless cover parliaments from six out of eight member states with regional parliaments with legislative powers. Only Portugal and Finland are missing, but both states combined only have three legislative regions. The results of the survey thus provide a general overview over the main organizational features of regional parliamentary administrations.

In a second phase, more detailed data was collected on the Belgian regional parliaments by means of qualitative interviews and documentary analysis. It has also been used to supplement the data from the questionnaire. Belgium was chosen as a case study as the Belgian regional parliaments have greater formal powers than their peers in other member states. In Declaration 51 attached to the TEU and the TFEU, the Kingdom of Belgium clarifies that its regional parliaments are to be considered as part of the national parliamentary system. This is based on the Belgian constitutional principle of *in foro interno in foro externo*, whereby those actors who are competent to act domestically on a certain subject matter are, by extension, also the actor in charge of external relations in that field. In practice, it means that the Belgian regions do not depend on the willingness of the national chambers to include their point of view (as is the case with other regional parliaments), but their reasoned opinions are to be forwarded in their original form to the European institutions. Thus, for example, as the Belgian regions have exclusive domestic competence in most aspects of environmental policy-making, subsidiarity tests in the field of environment policy are predominantly the task of the regional parliaments. At the same time, despite their greater formal powers, the Belgian subnational parliaments have not made much use of the EWS. Only the Flemish Parliament has adopted an opinion and a reasoned opinion so far. Hence, the case also shows that formal powers alone do not explain the level of activity of a parliament, and it raises the question as to what other factors and challenges play a role.

Finally, the insights into the Belgian system are compared with recent research on Scotland and the German Länder, in order to highlight some of the main similarities and differences in the organization of EU affairs scrutiny and the role of administrators therein. The comparison also allows us to better understand the challenges faced by different regional parliaments.

A first look at the staff resources of regional parliaments with legislative powers in the field of European affairs (Table 6.1) already highlights one of the fundamental challenges for regional parliaments in EU policy-making: their staff resources are extremely low. The vast majority of parliaments appear to have between one and three members of staff working on EU affairs. By comparison, there are only four out of 41 chambers of national parliaments that employ three or fewer staff members: both Slovenian chambers, Malta and the Dutch Senate – two of the smallest EU member states and a part-time upper house. The average across the regional parliaments that responded is about 1.7 staff

Table 6.1 Staff resources of regional parliaments in European affairs (2013)

		Number of staff*	**Increase of staff after Lisbon**
Austria	Burgenland	1	No
	Steiermark	N.i.	No
	Vorarlberg	1	No
	Wien	Normal staff**	No
Belgium	Brussels Parliament	1	N.i.
	Flemish Parliament	2–2.5	N.i.
	Francophone community	1	No
	German-speaking community	0.5	Yes
	Wallonia	2	+ 1
Germany	Berlin	3	+ 1
	Bremen	1	No
	Hessen	1	Yes, creation of the unit European and International Affairs
	Meck.-Vorpommern	3	Yes
	Sachsen	0.5	No
Italy	Trentino-Alto Adige	1	No
	Veneto	3	No
Spain	Andalucía	3	Reallocation of tasks between staff
	Galicia	Normal staff**	No
	Madrid	1	No
	Extremadura	2	No
	Valencia	n.i.	No
United Kingdom	Scotland	3.5	No
	Northern Ireland	1	No

*The number of staff does not include EU officers posted in Brussels.
**'Normal staff' means that the parliament has no specialized staff for EU affairs and that EU affairs are being dealt with by the staff that is responsible for domestic affairs.
Source: The table is primarily based on written questionnaires addressed to the EU administrations of the regional parliaments and supplemented with interview data.

members per parliament. The difference to national parliaments is striking. National parliaments employ on average about 9.8 EU staff. The difference is particularly striking at the higher end: the German Bundestag employs 44.5 EU staff, for example, whereas the best-staffed respondent among regional parliaments (Scotland) employed 3.5 (cf. Högenauer and Christiansen 2015).

If it is sometimes challenging for national parliaments to work through the flood of EU-related documents that they automatically receive due to improved information rights after Lisbon, low staff numbers mean that it is even more difficult for regional parliaments to identify important documents and to analyse the precise implications of the proposed policies for their country or region. In order to increase their capacity for proactive handling of EU affairs, about half of the parliaments that responded to the written questionnaire offered additional training on EU affairs to staff – for example, through the Subsidiarity Monitoring Network of the Committee of the Regions.

Another way to address the combined problem of the information flood and limited in-house expertise is to rely, at least to some extent, on the much better-staffed ministries of the regional executive. Whether such cooperation happens depends on the nature and quality of the relationship between the regional government and parliament more generally. In the case of Vienna and six out of 16 German Länder, for example, the regional executive frequently sends its own assessment of the subsidiarity question to the regional parliament, which can use it as guidance (cf. Häsing and Buzogany 2013; Högenauer 2016). In the case of Scotland, both the UK government and the Scottish government provide the Scottish Parliament with subsidiarity assessments. The advantage of this cooperation is that it reduces the work load of parliamentary staff: the EU experts of the Scottish parliament, for example, normally only review those proposals that have been identified as problematic by the regional or national government (Interview 1). As this affects only a minority of proposals (c.f. Chapter 5), it saves a great deal of time. The disadvantage is, however, that the assessments of the governments tend to be based on a narrow legal interpretation of the principle of subsidiarity (e.g. based on competences), which means that far fewer proposals are retained compared with parliaments such as the Swedish parliament that apply a more political interpretation of the principle of subsidiarity (Interview 1). Another potential disadvantage is that the parliaments risk becoming very reactive players that only act if others push them, instead of proactively analysing EU proposals for their compatibility with regional concerns.

Similar differences in regional culture can be observed in the level of cooperation between the regional offices in Brussels and regional parliaments. As noted earlier, unlike their national counterparts, the vast majority of regional parliaments cannot afford to send a permanent representative to Brussels. By contrast, most regional executives have a Brussels office, and some of the offices of the stronger legislative regions have enough staff to allow them to specialize in different policy areas (Högenauer 2014). Just as in the case of regional governments themselves, the offices of regional governments are sometimes willing to support their parliament – and sometimes not. In eight out of 23 cases, regional parliamentary administrations or interviewees reported that the regional (government) offices in Brussels provided them directly with information on EU issues (cf. Table 6.2). As some regions did not comment on this question, the extent of cooperation is probably being underestimated here. The precise form of cooperation varies. Sometimes the office offers advice specifically on the EWS, as in the case of the Burgenland and Steiermark. Sometimes, members of the regional office visit the parliaments. In that case, frequencies vary substantially. The Walloon attaché to the Belgian Permanent Representation estimates that he visits the Walloon parliament and the Parliament of the Francophone Community about once a year (Interview 2). The head of the office of Mecklenburg-West Pomerania estimates that he visits the parliament about every six weeks (Interview 3). In the case of Scotland, by contrast, the regional office stated explicitly that it does *not* provide information directly to the parliament, as it is the office of the government (Interview 4). However, while such cooperation with the government can have the positive result of reinforcing regional capacity to scrutinize European actors, it is a double-edged sword. It also has the side-effect of increasing the dependence of regional parliaments on their executives and, hence, of decreasing their capacity for effective control of their government in EU affairs.

Another area where differences between the national and the regional level are striking is the dispatching of parliamentary representatives to Brussels. As Neuhold and Högenauer (2013) show, all national parliaments but two have at least one administrator in Brussels who acts as parliamentary representative (see also Chapter 3). All of these representatives, except for the Germans, are based in one corridor in the EP building. On the one hand, this immensely facilitates access to the European institutions and to first-hand information but, on the other, it also allows the representatives to coordinate the work of national parliaments. In fact, they meet on a weekly basis to discuss European developments and parliamentary reactions, and informal meetings during the week are easy due to the close proximity of the offices (Neuhold and Högenauer 2013).

The regional parliaments have, by and large, not been able to emulate this system. Only two of the respondents had a representative

Table 6.2 Regional parliaments receiving information from the EU office (2013)

Country	Region	Role of regional government representative
Austria	Burgenland	Advice on EWS
	Steiermarck	Advice on EWS
Belgium	French Community	Visits parliament 1 per year
	Wallonia	Visits parliament 1 per year
Germany	Mecklenburg-Vorpommern	Offers advice to parliament
	Sachsen	Offers advice to parliament
Italy	Consiglio Regionale del Trentino-Alto Adige	Offers advice to parliament
Spain	Galicia	Offers advice to parliament

Source: Questionnaires addressed to the EU administrations of the regional parliaments and interview data.

in Brussels. A third region – Scotland – used to have a parliamentary representative but has effectively abolished this position by now (Högenauer 2016; Interviews 1 and 4). If we move beyond the survey, it is known that five of the 16 German Landtage have a representative in Brussels – that is, slightly less than one third of the Länder. Among these are mainly regions that are regarded as relatively large and/or politically strong: Bavaria, Baden-Württemberg, Hesse, Northrhine-Westphalia and Brandenburg (Interview 3). The functions of that network are similar to those of the national parliamentary representatives: to collect information at the source and to exchange information among each other. They also meet once a week in Brussels and maintain close contact with the representative of the German Bundestag in Brussels (Häsing and Buzogany 2013). Overall, however, given the generally low level of resources available to regional parliaments, it is unlikely that a genuine inter-parliamentary network of representatives will emerge in Brussels.

Few people, many tasks

Despite the much lower staff resources, the EU staff of regional parliaments perform the same range of tasks as the staff of national parliaments and the same typology applies (cf. Chapter 1). Even the proportion of regional parliamentary administrations performing a specific task tends to be similar to the proportion of national parliamentary administrations that perform this task. (cf. Table 6.3). Thus, in the

Table 6.3 Roles of parliamentary administrations at a glance (2013)

Region	Filtering	Procedural advice	Content advice	Drafting
Burgenland	Yes	Yes	By request	Sometimes
Steiermark	N.i.	N.i.	N.i.	By request
Vorarlberg	Yes	Yes	Yes	Yes
Vienna	Yes	N.i.	N.i.	N.i.
Francophone Community	Yes	Yes	Yes	Never used
Flanders	Yes	Yes	Yes	Yes, informally
Bruxelles	Yes	Yes	Not yet known	Never used
German-speaking Community	No	Yes	Yes	Never used
Wallonia	Yes	Yes	Yes	Yes
Berlin	Yes	Yes	Yes	No
Bremen	No	Yes	No	No
Hessen	Yes	Yes	Limited	No
Mecklenburg-West Pomerania	Yes	Yes	On request	On request
Saxony	No	On request	On request	On request
Trentino-Alto Adige	Yes	Yes	Yes	Yes
Veneto	Informally	Yes	No	Never used
Andalucía	No	Yes	No	Never used
Galicia	No	Yes	Limited	No
Madrid	Yes	Yes	Yes	To some extent
Extremadura	Yes	Yes	No	No
Valencia	No	Yes	Limited	Yes
Scotland	No	Yes	Yes	Yes
N. Ireland	Yes	Yes	Yes	Yes

Source: This table has been primarily based on data from the questionnaires, but supplemented with interview data where available.

case of national parliaments, 21 out of 28 parliamentary administrations (75 percent) covered by the survey sifted through the documents from the European and national level to preselect those that were deemed 'important' for further political discussion (cf. Chapter 5). In addition, the administration of the Austrian parliament conducted a form of preselection on the basis of tight political guidelines. In the case of regional parliaments, 15 out of the 22 parliamentary administrations in the study conducted such activities – that is, nearly 70 percent.

Similarly, as in the case of national parliaments, all administrations for which data is available advise MPs on the procedures available to them. Such procedural support is, of course, one of the traditional core tasks of parliamentary administrations but it is particularly important in European affairs, where politicians tend to be less familiar with the specificities of the European system. This also explains why about half of the administrations in the study were offered further training when the Lisbon Treaty introduced new procedures. Procedural advice allows administrators the opportunity to have potential influence on how a parliament reacts to an EU document, as they can emphasize available means of response.

Nearly 70 percent of regional parliamentary administrations also provide content-related advice (at least 16 out of 23), although several stress that the advice that they provide is 'limited'. Usually this means that they try to provide balanced or politically neutral advice, or that they try to focus on technical advice. This is actually slightly higher than in the case of national parliaments, where the figure lies at about 65 percent.

Finally, 12 out of 17 regional parliamentary administrations are involved in the drafting of (reasoned) opinions for the EWS or the political dialogue with the Commission, whereas five administrations never engage in this type of task. However, this is also type of task on which it is particularly difficult to obtain good information. All the other tasks – preselection, procedural advice and content-related advice – can be performed even if the parliaments do not actually adopt an opinion. However, in order for the administrations to know whether they would be involved in the *drafting* of an opinion, they either need a formal procedure that clearly allocates that task to them or an actual example where such a document was written. However, as discussed, 75 regional parliaments had only adopted 34 reasoned opinions by 2013. Hence, a large number of regional parliaments had never adopted a reasoned opinion or even an opinion for the political dialogue at the time of the study, which means that the question of drafting is very hypothetical. In addition, in 2013 several regional parliaments were still adapting their procedures in reaction to the Treaty of Lisbon, and even among existing formal procedures, the tasks of administrators are rarely specified in much detail. The rules of procedure of the parliament of the French-speaking community of Belgium are one of the few exceptions that specify the role of the administration (Règlement du Parlement de la communauté francophone, 13 July 2013). Taking into account the patchy participation of regional parliaments in the EWS, about 85 percent of national parliamentary administrations are involved in the drafting of opinions compared with about 70 percent of regional parliamentary administrations.

Thus, the overall pattern of work of regional parliamentary administrations looks very similar to that of national parliamentary administrations, despite much lower staff resources. But how can one interpret this? How is it that much smaller administrations apparently fulfil the same tasks as much larger administrations?

On the one hand, it means that regional parliamentary administrations – as national parliamentary administrations – perform tasks that go far beyond the technical: If an administration provides procedural advice 'proactively' – that is, actively reminds committee chairs or members that they have the power to do this or that on a certain issue – they are able not only facilitate the use of European procedures, but also to promote a certain culture of scrutiny. If, in addition, they provide advice on how the content of a European legislative proposal affects the region or on what exactly a proposal implies, they can to some extent influence the content and direction of the debate. If they are then also in charge of drafting the opinion, their ability to influence the outcome further is increased. And if they are formally or informally in charge of filtering European documents for relevance to begin with, they can to some extent influence the parliamentary agenda (cf. Högenauer and Neuhold 2013). This does not necessarily imply that administrators start to 'overrule' or 'manipulate' politicians, as the opportunities to shape the outcome depend also on the degree to which politicians trust their administrations. However, it means that the supportive role of the administration in the process leading up to an opinion is actually quite considerable and provides them with opportunities to try and convince politicians to act in certain ways. By extension, one can conclude that the extent to which a parliament functions effectively in EU policy-making also depends on the knowhow and motivation of its staff, as well as the availability of staff support in general.

This is where one has to look at the other side of the coin. While regional parliamentary administrations perform practically the same tasks as the administrations of national parliaments, their capacity to perform each task tends to be lower. This is reflected in the tendency of the administrations to nuance their precise role. Thus, most of the administrations of regional parliaments that provide content-related advice to the MPs stress that they either only provide advice if MPs ask for it, or stress the technical and limited nature of the advice they provide. Similarly, half of the administrations say that they only participate in the drafting of documents *on request*. In other words, many regional parliamentary administrations do not perform their tasks *proactively*, but *reactively*, if and when MPs approach them. However, one statement that comes up time and again is that many parliamentary administrations feel that EU affairs scrutiny works best if the administration plays a proactive role and actively identifies important issues, points potential problems out to MPs and suggests possible courses of action (cf. Interview 5; also Chapter 5).

Functions of and challenges for parliamentary administrations: Belgium

As mentioned previously, the Belgian sub-national parliaments have greater formal powers under the EWS than any other regional parliament. Based on Declaration 51 attached to the European Treaties and on the Belgian constitutional principle of *in foro interno in foro externo*, they are responsible for the subsidiarity tests in those policy areas that fall under their competence domestically. Yet, the EWS cannot simply be applied to sub-national parliaments: under the EWS, each national parliament has two votes and, in the case of bicameral parliaments, each chamber has one vote. When the votes are added up at the European level to ascertain whether the threshold for a yellow or orange card has been reached, the counting is done in terms of full votes, not fractions of a vote. In the Belgian case, however, if a competence is located at the sub-national level, there will be at least three parliaments that are competent to act – the Flemish parliament, the Walloon parliament and the Brussels parliament, or the Flemish parliament, the parliament of the francophone community and the parliament of the German-speaking community. If a competence is shared between the federal and sub-national level, there could be even more parliaments involved – for example, five regional and federal chambers. Thus, in order to be compatible with the EU's expectations of how the EWS functions, a system had to be found where the different voices could be added up in such a way that either no vote, 1 vote or 2 votes were cast (and not 0.2, 0.67 votes or 1.33 votes).

This system is defined in the Belgian cooperation agreement concerning the exercise of the competences of national parliaments accorded by the Treaty of Lisbon (Ontwerp van samenwerkingsakkoord 7 and 9 July 2008). Article 6 endorses a system whereby subsidiarity concerns have a greater weight than the absence of concerns (cf. Article 6 and Interview 5). Hence, as a general rule, as soon as one competent parliament adopts a reasoned opinion, this results in a vote being cast (even if it is only one out of three or one out of five competent parliaments). If two sub-national parliaments from different linguistic regimes raise concerns in an area of exclusive regional competence, both votes are cast. If a competence is shared between the federal and the sub-national levels, two votes are cast if at least one federal chamber and one regional parliament raise concerns.

Normally, cooperation agreements have a quasi-constitutional status in Belgium. However, in this case, the cooperation agreement has been signed but not ratified, which means that it has not yet entered into effect. It is nevertheless being treated as a gentlemen's agreement and its system is already being followed (Interview 5).

Due to the European rules and expectations with regard to the EWS, all information coming from the European level is communicated to the Belgian parliaments via a single email address managed by the Senate. The documents are then forwarded to all parliaments at the same time. Each parliament has to assess on its own whether it deems that a document falls under its competences. Ultimately, all reasoned opinions have to be communicated to the European level via the federal parliament (Interview 5).

What happens between the transmission of the European documents and the final transmission of a reasoned opinion differs somewhat between parliaments, as each parliament has adopted its own procedure – for example, Flanders in 2013, Brussels in 2014 and so on. However, there are some commonalities. For instance, in most Belgian parliaments the committee in charge of a dossier seems to be the relevant sectoral committee (e.g. environment) rather than a dedicated European affairs committee. However, as only the Flemish parliament has ever adopted a reasoned opinion, the precise dynamics on the political level are still somewhat in flux. Even in the Flemish case, for instance, the adoption of the reasoned opinion diverged from the formal rules: instead of a discussion in the committee followed by a decision by the plenary, the opinion was discussed and adopted directly in the plenary (Interview 5). The roles of the EU staff are, however, quite similar across parliaments.

The Flemish parliament is slightly better-staffed than its peers. It has one full-time EU clerk, a member of the legal service who covers EU issues among other things, and a secretary and a member of technical staff (for the website) who spend part of their time on EU issues. The staff has by now gained some experience with the procedures. The parliament participated in two subsidiarity tests in 2006 or 2007 as part of the subsidiarity monitoring network to test the new procedures and then adopted a reasoned opinion and an opinion in 2013 (Interview 5). On the whole, they feel that the staff resources are sufficient for the moment, but only to respond to demand from politicians. Hence, the feeling is that:

> If we had more people, we could try to stimulate the debate more. I often have to take the initiative to stimulate activities, and with more people, you could do more.
>
> (ibid)

However, out of 300 staff at the Flemish parliament, only about 30–40 people have a university background. As a result, 'there is not much knowhow. We need to invite people from the Flemish administration and other experts to get more knowhow and information on EU issues' (Interview 5; cf. Interview 6, for similar views).

This relates to a common phenomenon among regional parliaments – namely, that their EU staff tends to be more reactive than proactive than that of national parliaments due to low staff numbers. In the Belgian case, the staff generally deplores not being able to act more proactively, because their parliaments face an additional challenge: Belgian MPs are generally seen to be pro-European and thus to lack a 'scrutiny reflex' with regard to EU affairs (Interview 6). In other words, many MPs are so pro-European that they find it unnecessary to scrutinize EU policy proposals too closely, or that they perceive this as being an EU-critical act. In addition, there is a feeling that European outcomes often tend to be similar to what Belgium would do anyway (Interview 7). The result of the combination of lack of political motivation and low staff resources is thus that it is difficult to establish an active scrutiny culture.

In terms of precise tasks, the Flemish administration generally offers all MPs all information that falls into the competences of the parliament (Interview 5). However, posting this information on a committee website usually does not trigger a political response. Thus, in addition, the staff monitors the main proposals in the Commission Work Programme and the priorities of the SMN more specifically. In addition, they try to spot topics that could be controversial in Flanders – for example, the Ports Directive, which gave rise to the Flemish reasoned opinion. In order to raise political awareness of these topics, the staff then try to invite MEPs, ministers or other visitors for further discussion. They try to convince the committee chairs or they distribute the reasoned opinions of other regional parliaments from the REGPEX website for inspiration. That also reduces the politicians' fear of the technicalities of subsidiarity questions (Interview 5). Hence, for issues that are deemed important, the Flemish parliamentary administration tries to develop a system of preselection and advice.

The role of the administration at the stage where reasoned opinions are drafted can only be assessed for the Flemish parliament, where this case arose (cf. Figure 6.2). Here, the initial drafting was done by the administration so far, with party staff or MPs writing the final version. However, the EU staff feels that ideally party staff or the assistants of MPs should be in charge of the drafting, on the basis of a list of pro and contra arguments supplied by the administration (Interview 5).

In the Parliament of the francophone community, only one administrator works on EU affairs. She initially selects the documents on the basis of the title, and then on the basis of their first page. The interesting documents are then read in further detail and included in the bulletin to the MPs. Each committee has a *Europromoteur* – that is, an

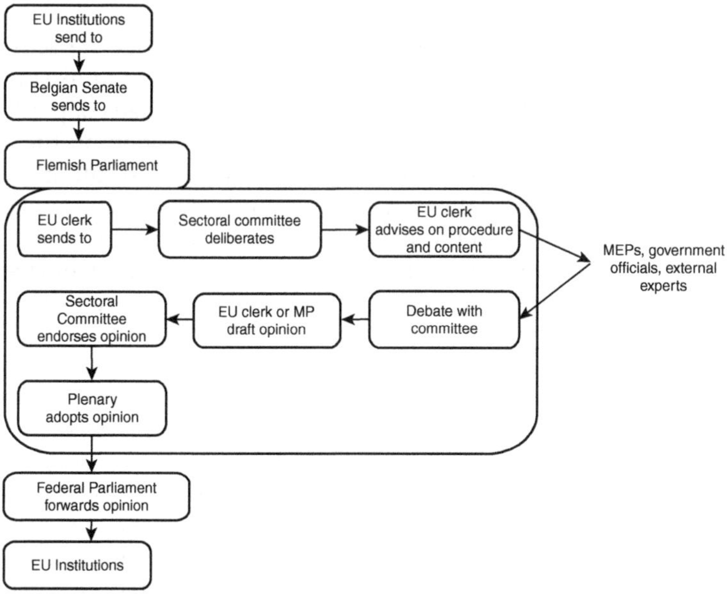

Figure 6.2 Adoption of opinions in the Flemish parliament*
Note: *The precise procedure within the Flemish parliament will vary somewhat from case to case, depending on the characteristics of the dossier and the people involved.
Source: Compiled by the author, based on Interview 5.

MP who is responsible for following EU issues in the area of expertise of the committee. This person is an important contact point for the official, as the Europromoteur can propose to put certain issues on the agenda of the committee. The administrator thus also tries to play the role of motivator, together with the Europromoteurs, by selecting potentially interesting dossiers. As with all Belgian parliaments, there are some concerns about the lack of interest in EU affairs among politicians, but she also feels that the absence of reasoned opinions is at least in part related to the fact that the competences of the communities do not include many areas where the EU can adopt 'hard' laws. In her view, there are only about five to six interesting dossiers per year (Interview 6).

In the case of the parliament of the Brussels regions, the procedure for subsidiarity tests was not created until March 2014. Their one staff member, who works on EU affairs only part of his time, sends a newsletter every second week that includes all new legislative proposals. Unlike his colleagues in other parliaments, he selects the dossiers primarily based on competence, not on potential interest. But he also estimates that there are only about ten proposals per year that affect the region (Interview 7).

A role that all the clerks have in common is that they are actively involved in inter-parliamentary cooperation. Interestingly, unlike in the German case (cf. Häsing and Buzogany 2013), intra-Belgian cooperation is limited (Interview 7). This is at least in part a reflection on the fact that the right to diversity plays a greater role in the federalization of the Belgian state than in the cooperative German system. In Germany, the Landtage need to find a majority in the Bundesrat to be able to voice their subsidiarity concerns in a reasoned opinion. As discussed previously, in Belgium, one single parliament is enough to cast a vote at the European level.

In Belgium, the clerks of the various parliaments come together once a year to evaluate past activities and discuss potential problems. They also have a list of their colleagues in other Belgian parliaments, so that they can enter into direct contact (Interview 6). However, this cooperation is not formal and cannot be compared with the Austrian efforts, where regional parliaments and their administrations specialize on certain policy areas and exchange views with their counterparts (Interview 5).

However, in the absence of a network of parliamentary representatives who specialize on cooperation, the EU affairs staff of the regional parliaments play a more active role in inter-parliamentary cooperation. The EU expert of the parliament of Brussels, for example, attends all meetings of the SMN, which take place in Brussels anyway. He is also involved in CALRE meetings, which are good for networking. He has, however, noticed two barriers to effective intra-parliamentary cooperation between regions: first, *all* parliaments have limited staff and hence limited knowhow on European policy issues. Second, there is a language barrier, which is again stronger on the level of regional parliaments than on the level of national parliaments. In several cases, not only the politicians, but also the administrators speak little English. As a result, even just organizing a meeting over the phone can be a challenge (Interview 7).

A final task of parliamentary administrations is often to organize the reform of internal procedures regarding subsidiarity. Thus, the Scottish administration was in charge of creating and piloting a new system of scrutiny tests when the old system was deemed too slow (Högenauer 2016). Similarly, the EU staff of the Brussels parliament played an active role in the creation of the new procedure in 2014. For this purpose, the clerk consulted existing procedures in Belgium and then also took into account the procedures of other regional parliaments, provided that they were available in a suitable language. He then discussed the details of the procedure with the president of the parliament, who also fed her ideas into the process. The procedure was then formally adopted by the bureau (Interview 7). In the case of the parliament of the francophone community, the EU staff also played an active role in the evolution of the procedures. In 2009, the administrator took the initiative to inform the MPs through a newsletter, once every two weeks, of new EU documents (Interview 6).

Conclusion

To conclude, the analysis of the administrations of regional parliaments and their role in EU affairs has shown that regional parliaments have, in general, only a fraction of the staff resources that are available to national parliaments. Despite this fact, their administrations generally endeavour to perform the same functions in EU affairs scrutiny as the administrations of national parliaments. This leads to three main concluding observations.

First, the roles of the administrations of regional parliaments are not limited to technical tasks but include a wide range of activities that allow administrators to shape the process of scrutiny through selection and advice. This supports the argument that legislatures – like executives – are also bureaucratic actors, despite the fact that they are often treated as purely political actors in the literature (cf. Christiansen et al. 2014).

Second, while the extent of administrative involvement could be problematic in cases of violation of trust and political neutrality, it is nevertheless a crucial element of the scrutiny process. The fact that parliaments are at a relative disadvantage compared with the much bigger ministries has often been stressed (Christiansen et al. 2014). European policy-making adds a new layer of complexity with its different procedures. Thus, in order to keep up with the executives, legislatures are required to rely on their (much smaller) administrations. This analysis, as well as similar analyses of national parliaments, shows that administrations play an important role in sorting information and in alerting politicians to potentially problematic or relevant developments (cf. Högenauer and Neuhold 2013; Winzen 2014).

Third, despite their attempts at fulfilling a wide range of roles in coordination, reform, preselection, advice and so on, regional parliamentary administrations struggle to support their parliaments to the extent to which they would like to support them. Due to low staff numbers, existing staff is often forced to *react* to demands from politicians, where they would like to be able to inform them more proactively on a regular basis. One of the effects is a risk that regional parliaments can exercise parliamentary control of EU affairs only in cooperation with their executives, which then, in turn, reduces the ability of parliaments to exercise their control function vis-à-vis their government.

Thus, the general picture is mixed: the wave of EU-related reforms within regional parliaments demonstrates that there is an ambition to engage actively with EU affairs. Similarly, the efforts of parliamentary administrations to fulfil a range of roles point towards an eagerness to support such an ambition. However, given the low resources of regional parliaments, it is possible that these efforts will not reach a limit. In light of this dilemma (high expectations, low resources), it seems legitimate for regional parliaments to explore new ways of increasing capacity, even if cooperation with regional governments on subsidiarity tests may create some form of dependency. After all, it may simply not be possible to recreate in an exact manner forms of scrutiny, control and consultation at ever-lower levels of government.

Interviews

Interview 1: EAC clerk, Scottish Parliament, 1 April 2015.

Interview 2: Walloon attaché in the Belgian Permanent Representation, 7 April 2014.

Interview 3: Regional Office, Mecklenburg-West Pomerania, 2 April 2014.

Interview 4: Interview with the SGOEU, 8 April 2014.

Interview 5: Two officials, Flemish parliament, 2 April 2014.

Interview 6: Clerk, Parliament of the francophone community, 30 April 2014.

Interview 7: Clerk, Brussels parliament, 22 May 2014.

Conclusion

The analysis conducted in the preceding chapters has demonstrated the variety of roles which parliamentary administrators carry out in the management of EU affairs. Our analysis has shown that, at every level in the EU's multilevel parliamentary system, administrators are involved not only as assistants of the political players, but also as analysts, advisors and potentially as agenda-setters. In addition, the coordination of the parliamentary dimension of EU affairs – whether within individual chambers, or between the legislatures of different member states, or indeed across levels – often puts administrators in the spotlight.

Keeping in mind that parliaments are not unitary actors, and that in the EU context such horizontal and vertical coordination between different parliaments is becoming more and more important, the role of administrators has become essential in Europe. Managing the growing influx of documents and dossiers that national parliaments receive from the European level, communicating their substance effectively to MPs, facilitating the formation of opinion within and across the various chambers and coordinating, as far as possible, the collective response of national parliaments has become a massive challenge for parliaments – putting the spotlight on the capacity, expertise and skills of administrators.

Our research demonstrates that the administrative capacities of national parliaments vary significantly across the EU. The EP stands out as an institution with significant administrative support – it is the biggest parliament in Europe, and has a comparatively sizeable administration. The emphasis in the EP, as in most national parliaments, is on providing administrative support to political groups, to the various committees and to the institution as a whole. This is in contrast to the experience of the US Congress, where individual congressmen and -women have a much greater number of staff than the two to three assistants and interns that work for MEPs.

In Chapter 2, we showed how significant the contribution of parliamentary staff is for the effective functioning of the EP, by illustrating the roles that they play through a number of specific cases. These examples demonstrated that there is a significant amount of delegation from MEPs to parliamentary staff, and that these fulfil a variety of roles. Through their analysis of legislative proposals, through the coordination of responses from different political groups and through their assistance in the drafting of parliamentary reports and opinions, the committee secretariats of the EP assist the opinion-formation process inside the institution. In doing so, they also strengthen the capacity of the EP in its relations with other institutions – an important consideration in view of the fact that, despite all its political power, the EP is often at a disadvantage vis-à-vis the Council and the Commission with respect to resources, expertise and time.

National parliaments are arguably even more under pressure when it comes to meeting the challenges of European integration. The focus of MPs and political parties is predominantly on domestic issues – areas in which parliaments have legislative and budgetary authority, on which there is greater media attention and, consequently, greater promise of electoral recognition. Even though European integration has, over time, become a more salient issue in many member states, and there are now frequent debates on issues with a European dimension, there is usually little electoral gain from focusing on the details of the EU dossiers on which parliaments are being consulted.

In addition, such dossiers are usually complex, requiring expertise not only on the technical substance involved, but also on the procedural issues of EU decision-making. Furthermore, national parliaments in the EU cannot act effectively on their own; they require cooperation among several chambers in order to make an impact on EU decision-making. Thus, before taking up an issue in one parliament – investing the time and political resources required in order to politicize it – it will be helpful to be aware of reactions and the potential for action in the parliaments of other member states.

As the discussion in Chapters 3 and 4 has shown, national parliaments rely to a large extent on administrators to support internal opinion-formation and facilitate external cooperation. Administrators assigned either to individual committees or to central coordination units are tasked with managing the influx of material from Brussels, with filtering out relevant dossiers and with alerting elected politicians to possible action that may be required. Chapter 4 shows that some national parliaments have increased their human resources following the Lisbon Treaty in order to deal with the greater administrative demand that has come with the introduction of the EWS but, in many cases, staff levels have remained unchanged or – in a few cases – have even declined in the wake of the financial crisis.

Lack of resources is therefore one possible explanation for the limited response that national parliaments have had to the EWS, with only two 'yellow cards' issued in the first five years of the system being in operation. As is well-known by now, the uptake of the new powers has been rather selective across the member states, with only a minority of national parliaments accounting for the majority of reasoned opinions that have been issued. Beyond the formal powers of national parliaments and the political saliency of the particular issues under discussion, the administrative support available for EU affairs is an important factor in explaining this divergence.

In regional parliaments, the situation is generally exacerbated by the fewer resources and greater distance to EU decision-making that prevails there. As Chapter 6 discussed, there is great variation among the regional parliaments, both in terms of their involvement in EU affairs and with respect to their administrative capacity. Individual regional parliaments, in regions with legislative powers or within federal states, have procedures and resources to engage with EU affairs on a regular basis but, on the whole, the small administrations of regional parliaments make it difficult for these to be proactive about EU matters.

Inter-parliamentary cooperation has seen a significant increase in the years after the Lisbon Treaty, both in terms of national parliaments working with the EU institutions and through horizontal cooperation with one another. This is building on the long-standing efforts of the COSAC Secretariat which has been facilitating the bi-annual Conference of Parliamentary Committees for Union Affairs of Parliaments of the European Union. The COSAC Secretariat, established in 2004, also maintains the records of the Conference, compiles and publishes its bi-annual reports, and plays a key role in supporting the COSAC Presidency in exercising its role.

However, since the mid-1990s, in addition to the continuing efforts of COSAC, a growing number of individual parliaments dispatched their own representatives to Brussels. Located usually not within the permanent representations of the member states but, rather, within the premises of the EP, these NPRs provide the hinge between the European and the national levels of parliamentary involvement in EU affairs. Working with their institutions in the national capitals, the NPRs facilitate a two-way flow of information, bringing EU developments to the attention of colleagues at the national level, but also 'uploading' domestic concerns and priorities to the EU.

As Chapter 3 demonstrated, the NPRs have also formed a close bureaucratic network among themselves, providing an opportunity for horizontal information exchange about the scrutiny of EU affairs being conducted within their respective chambers. Through regular meetings, NPRs update each other on developments within the member states and thereby make possible the swift identification of areas of common concern. It is this 'short-circuiting' of national agendas that underpins efforts to achieve the required numbers of reasoned opinions among member states, notwithstanding the need for political agreement that such initiatives require.

The example of the NPRs shows that, beyond merely gathering information and advising politicians, administrators can also have an influence on taking initiatives, thereby indirectly contributing to the agenda-setting within and among national parliaments. An NPR reporting to their capital that MPs in several other member states are considering the launch of a reasoned opinion has the potential to mobilize political action also by their own parliament – a pattern that emphasizes the political influence that administrators can have, whether they are operating at the European or the national level.

The research presented in this volume therefore demonstrates that the parliamentarization of European integration – the increasing power of the EP, the growing role of national parliaments and the rise of interparliamentary cooperation among them – has triggered a corresponding process of bureaucratization. Parliaments are increasingly relying on support from administrators, albeit to varying degrees and in different ways. As the scrutiny of EU decision-making has become a greater concern for parliaments, the involvement of – and, indeed, the reliance on – administrators to facilitate these scrutiny mechanisms has increased. Effective scrutiny requires competent administrative support; this, in turn, facilitates – under certain conditions – an agenda-setting role for civil servants steering the process of political decision-making.

However – and this is an important conclusion from a normative perspective – we have found no evidence that bureaucrats are 'taking over'. This is also the case for the EP where, although we found that officials can adopt a 'steering role', the final decision in the cases under scrutiny is still taken by members of the European Parliament (MEPs). Also within national parliaments, administrators play a substantial role in a majority of parliaments by way of providing both procedural and content advice. Ultimate control and the final say has remained, however, in the hands of elected politicians, and whether a political party, a parliamentary committee or, indeed, an entire chamber takes issue with EU draft legislation is a political not an administrative decision. Our systematic research into the administration of EU scrutiny, albeit based on a limited number of selected case studies, has not brought any signs of 'bureaucratic drift' to light, and there is no parliamentary equivalent of the principal-agent problems that often characterize the political-bureaucratic divide in the executive branch.

At the outset of this volume, we pointed to the paradox of parliaments relying on bureaucracies for their functioning. In the light of our research, however, we can conclude that there is no normative conflict between parliamentary activity and its administrative support. On the whole, parliamentary administrators bring EU matters to the attention of their political masters, perhaps influencing matters somewhat by highlighting certain dossiers over others and helping to build transnational coalitions in the context of the EWS. But there is no danger that we can see that this bureaucratic element, in the process, takes over and might determine the outcome of the scrutiny process. If anything, there is a sense that administrators, dealing with EU matters in national parliaments, do not succeed sufficiently often in bringing such matters to a large enough audience of MPs, and that with the focus of political priorities lying elsewhere, opportunities for greater EU involvement by national parliaments are being missed.

Overall, the nascent research on the role of officials, both within the EP and within national parliaments, highlights the crucial role that administrators play – at least, under certain conditions. In the case of the EP we already noted that administrators can assume a steering role, even in fields that are traditionally considered as being of high political importance. In national parliaments, officials have been described as playing an advisory role in EU affairs and, as such, at times come up with concrete solutions. At the European level, we see the emergence of a network of (parliamentary) officials endeavouring to enhance parliamentary scrutiny.

While the Lisbon Treaty and the introduction of the EWS have created new opportunities – and challenges – for national parliaments and their administrations, this development has been overlaid, if not eclipsed, by the impact of the sovereign debt crisis in the Eurozone. For the national parliaments of the member states in the Eurozone, this created new pressures of having to deal with European matters of high complexity on a regular basis. This has been the case for both creditors and debtor countries: parliaments in the programme countries have had to make difficult and painful decisions about the acceptance of cuts and reform demands from the troika institutions, while parliaments in the donor states had to weigh the costs of repeated bail-outs. For both sides, this not only involved tough political choices, but also required new expertise in the technical details of Eurozone financial policy-making.

Much has been made of the 'technocratic' handling of the debt crisis in the Eurozone, and the imposition of neoliberal preferences of European and international creditors, leaving programme countries with little influence over the reforms required of them in return for bail-out disbursements. Yet, in the context of the Greek crisis in 2015, the primacy of political decision-making over technocratic considerations also asserted itself, and images of the Greek Parliament became iconic during the height of the crisis. The chambers of the Greek, the German, and of many other national parliaments turned not only into important fora for debate over the future of Europe, but were also the place were crucial votes took place that defined the direction of future developments. In this period, too, the EP witnessed some of the most high-profile debates of its history.

The crisis required parliaments to become involved in highly salient decision-making in EU affairs, thereby putting additional demands on their expertise in a very technical, yet also politically sensitive, domain. The Eurozone crisis has also been particularly difficult to handle from an institutional perspective because it is clearly a European issue that required a coordinated national response. Affecting mainly the Eurozone members rather than the EU as a whole, and requiring bail-outs from national sources rather than from the EU budget, the crisis limited the role of the EP and elevated the European dimension of national parliamentary work.

Due to these particularities, the Eurozone crisis emphasized the challenge in inter-level cooperation between the European and the national parliaments. On the one hand, there is the need to work together, not least in new institutional mechanisms such as the inter-parliamentary conference set up by the Fiscal Compact. On the other hand, there is the potential for institutional competition, if not rivalry, between the two levels concerning future arrangements for the scrutiny of Eurozone decision-making. While this potential conflict pitches one set of politicians (from the EP) against another (from national parliaments), it is often left to administrators to make sure that effective cooperation can take place against this background.

The need for cooperation – and the presence of tensions – between parliaments in Europe on different territorial levels have not only been confined to fiscal and monetary matters. Another inter-parliamentary conference has been set up in the area of foreign and security policy, and there the number of joint committee meetings in a range of policy areas has risen. Such structured cooperation between the European and the national parliament has become a mainstay of parliamentary work in the EU and, as such, also makes new demands on administrators. In some cases, the infrastructure being provided is that of the EP while, in others, the host institution rotates in line with the EU presidency, putting the respective national parliament in charge.

These developments demonstrate not only the growing parliamentarization of European integration, and the presence of a multilevel parliamentary system, they also indicate the pressures towards ever-greater cooperation across different levels. This includes the three levels discussed in this volume – regional, national and European – but, in fact, goes beyond these and also includes the growing practice of global inter-regional parliamentary cooperation. Examples such as the Euro-Latin American Parliamentary Assembly, composed of an equal number of MEPs and members of regional parliaments from Latin America, or the Asia-Europe Parliamentary Partnership Meeting, bringing together parliamentarians from the ASEM member states and from the EP, are cases in point.

Parliamentary work in Europe may still be dominated by a focus on domestic issues, but there is an ever-stronger European and transnational dimension to the activities of European parliaments. In a continent in which governments work more closely together across a range of policy-areas, though without necessarily delegating competences to common institutions, national parliaments have become an essential part of scrutinizing such cooperation. In the final conclusion, this demands from parliaments the capacity to hold national executives to account, to cooperate systematically with one another in a transnational context and also to build up effective links across the various territorial levels.

As we have seen in this volume, these demands can only be met if parliaments and their component parts have sufficient administrative support. Effective scrutiny of EU affairs and systematic inter-parliamentary cooperation require capacities in terms of technical expertise, language skills and informal networks that are being provided, by and large, by officials and clerks rather than elected MPs. Yet, we have also found that administrators are working with or for elected politicians, rather than against them or behind their back. Coming back to the paradox mentioned earlier – namely, that parliaments seem to rely on bureaucrats – there does not appear to be a fundamental conflict between parliamentary democracy and increasing bureaucratization: quite the opposite, in fact. Following our analysis, we can observe that the reliance of MPs on the services of officials is actually becoming essential for an effective functioning of representative democracy. Or, to put it bluntly, in an integrated Europe representation is inextricably linked to bureaucratization.

For these reasons, it will be important to further develop the research agenda and to build on the insights that the present analysis and other recent contributions have provided. One important aspect of this work will need to be conceptual: development and applying new concepts that are capable of capturing the unique nature of parliamentary administrations – bureaucracies working within legislative institutions, providing the interface between internal decision-making and external cooperation. This volume has made a first contribution by identifying the different roles administrators may take up, and by conducting the empirical analysis on the way in which these roles matter in practice. Nevertheless, more work needs to be done in order fully to conceptualize the nature of this phenomenon. One way of approaching the question is the recourse to the literature on the US Congress and its staff. However, concepts developed within the American experience cannot simply be exported to the very particular institutional and normative context of the European Union.

This volume has shed light on a topic that hitherto received only scant attention. In doing so, it has also shown that the role played by unelected officials in European legislatures merits further exploration – it touches on key normative issues that are at the heart of further integration in Europe: the capacity of democratic institutions to hold executives at the European and the national levels to account. Consequently, the nature of parliamentary administrations, their influence on the political decision-making process and their effectiveness in supporting MPs in their relations with executives, deserve more sustained research efforts from the academic community.

In the future, the demands on both the EP and on national parliaments are likely to increase. A strong discourse for future EU reform is building around the idea that national parliaments should have greater powers to limit or block further integration. There have even been calls for parliaments – either collectively or even individually – to receive the right to show a 'red card' to proposed EU legislation.

Others go even further and push for national parliaments to be able to repeal or 'repatriate' European legislation which they consider inappropriate. Even if such proposals do not have widespread support, they will help to keep the spotlight on the role of parliaments in Europe – and on their administrations – in the coming years.

Notes

2 Administrative Players in the European Parliament

1. Neuhold and Dobbels (2014) 'Paper-keepers or Policy Shapers? The Role of Unelected Officials in the European Parliament', *Comparative European Politics*, doi:10.1057/cep.2014. Dobbels and Neuhold (2013) 'The Roles Bureaucrats Play: The Input of the European Parliament (EP) Administrators into the Ordinary Legislative Procedure: A Case Study Approach', *Journal of European Integration*, 35(4): pp. 375–90.
2. With regard to the methodological approach, we adhered to the method of process-tracing by way of description of trajectories of change and paying attention to sequence (Collier 2011).
3. In this endeavour, 25 interviews were conducted with officials from the three EU institutions (Commission, Council and EP) involved in the files under study. These involved the key players (administrators and MEPs) in the negotiations who worked closely with the 'unit of analysis', officials working for the EP committee secretariat, and these officials themselves. The interviews were carried out in 2011 and 2012 after the files under study had been concluded (Dobbels and Neuhold 2013).
4. For more detailed analysis of these negotiations, see Brandsma and Blom-Hansen (2012).
5. Nanotechnology makes it possible to manipulate structures at nanometric scale (one billionth of a metre). In practical terms, nanotechnology can, for instance, be used to change fat, sugar or salt levels while retaining the full taste (Mahoney 2010).
6. See Benedetto (2013), for an analysis that challenges the assumption that the EP and the Council are on an equal footing with regard to the budget.
7. The Committee has 21 days to negotiate a common text. If this fails, the Commission has to come up with a new draft budget. Once a text is agreed by the Conciliation Committee, both Council and Parliament have 14 days to approve or reject it. If by 1 January, the first day of the budgetary year, the budget has not been approved, the Union works with 1/12 each month of the budget of the year before.
8. Delegated acts are regulated in Article 290 of the Treaty on Functioning of the EU (TFEU) and it is stipulated that a legislative act may delegate to the Commission the amendment of certain non-legislative elements of general application, or the amendment or supplement of non-essential elements of the legislative acts.
9. Here, we build on Wlezien (2005) who argues that a distinction should be made between an issue and a problem. An issue is not salient or important *per se*, but it depends on the degree to which it is *perceived* as a political problem.

3 Transnational Bureaucratic Networks in the EU: The Role of Parliamentary Officials in Inter-parliamentary Coordination and Control

1. The position for the Slovak and Bulgarian parliament is currently vacant. This is, however, to be filled again.
2. Officials do attend and prepare inter-parliamentary meetings such as the Inter-parliamentary Conference on CFSP/CSDP or the Speakers Conference. These are, however, rather incidental forms of cooperation.
3. The questions asked ranged from the daily tasks that the respective NPRs fulfil to how they keep in touch with their respective national legislature, the nature of the regular meetings of NPRs (Monday Morning Meetings), the system of parliamentary scrutiny of the respective member states and the implications for staff.
4. These questionnaires were filled in by country experts as part of the OPAL Country Reports. They contained data on the date when the NPRs were established and the legal rules concerning NPRs. This data covers all EU member states.
5. In sum, these interviews were conducted during the period September 2010 to January 2015.
6. Moreover, the empirical conclusions and their conceptualization have been discussed at a so-called 'Monday Morning Meeting' of the NPRs to confirm the validity of the insights on 6 May 2013. Another presentation on the use of the Lisbon provisions by national parliaments was given to the representatives of national parliaments in Brussels in December 2014.
7. The Danish NPR was at this point, however, based at the Belgian Chamber of Representatives.
8. While at a given point in time not all positions are filled, this is temporary (e.g. Bulgaria and Slovakia do not have a representative).
9. Bill Cash, Open Lectures, House of Commons, London, 21 February 2013.
10. The German delegation is unique in that it has two dimensions: an administrative dimension and one in which the political party groups are represented; due to its size, it uses office space outside of the EP (Interview 14).
11. See, for example, the Seminar Engaging with Europe: Parliamentary Control in EU Affairs, organized by the Dutch Parliamentary Representation in Brussels, 11 December 2014. This seminar was preceded by a session between academics and NPRs to discuss practices of parliamentary control.
12. According to Article 10 of Protocol 1 on the Role of National Parliaments in the European Union of the Treaty of Lisbon.
13. The Protocol on the 'Role of National Parliaments in the European Union' of the Treaty of Amsterdam for the first time recognized COSAC. It came into force 1 May 1999.
14. Current, previous and subsequent Presidencies. In January 2015, this played out as follows: Latvia (Presidency of COSAC) appointed two officials (one is the Latvian NPR and the other is a parliamentary official), Italy appointed two members (one from each chamber) and Luxembourg appointed one official.

15. The Presidential Troika refers to the delegation of coordination tasks to NPRs of the previous, the current and the subsequent Presidencies, as well as the European Parliament (COSAC 2011, 2.5).
16. This is currently an official of the Cypriot House of Representatives.
17. When the respective national parliament assumed the Presidency.
18. In January 2015, the Permanent Member was an official from the Cypriot parliament supporting the Latvian Presidency.
19. In the period 2012–14, five plenary sessions of the IPC on CFSP/CSDP were held: Cyprus (Pafos), September 2012; Ireland (Dublin), March 2013; Lithuania (Vilnius), September 2013; Greece (Athens), April 2014; Italy (Rome), November 2014.
20. These meetings are held every Monday morning except during the EP plenary sessions in Strasbourg.
21. Proposal for a Council regulation on the exercise of the right to take collective action within the context of the freedom of establishment and the freedom to provide services, Brussels, 21 March 2012 COM(2012) 130 final.
22. The interviews are kept anonymous as requested by the interviewees.

4 The Administrations of National Parliaments and the Scrutiny of EU Affairs

1. Gailmard and Patty (2007) argue, for instance, that there is a dilemma in that bureaucrats are most likely to develop expertise in a given policy area if they are interested in the issues at stake. At the same time, this means that they usually have preferences of their own in these policy areas, which creates a risk of political bias.
2. Interviews were conducted in Germany, France, the UK, Italy, the Netherlands, Belgium, Denmark, Poland, Slovakia, Sweden, the Czech Republic and Romania.
3. Greer and Jarman (2011: 17) discuss, for example, how the expectation of impartiality can lead administrators in the British executive to implement radically different policies within just a few years.

5 The Europeanization of National Parliamentary Administrations: Convergence or Divergence?

1. This research was conducted in the framework of a larger project on national parliaments after Lisbon (OPAL).
2. Among the administration, interviews were primarily conducted with the EU advisors or clerks of the European affairs committee. In some cases, where sectoral committees play an important role in parliamentary scrutiny, interviews with sectoral committee staff were added. The interview questions covered the tasks of parliamentary administrations at different stages of the process, the interaction between parliamentary staff and politicians, party staff and MP assistants, the role of staff in inter-parliamentary cooperation and the key challenges for them and their parliaments in EU affairs.
3. This section on the Austrian parliament draws on Mastenbroek et al. (2014).

4. Each political group in the Austrian parliament has a political group advisor. These are responsible for both the Main Committee and the EU Subcommittee on EU Affairs. Within their realm of competence fall the upper and lower houses of the Austrian parliament (Bundesrat and Nationalrat) when dealing with EU issues.
5. This *jour fixe* is chaired and initiated by an official working for the second President of the Austrian Parliament.
6. In the Bundesrat, ministers do not need to attend meetings of the Bundesrat's EAC. The heads of units of ministries do attend meetings of the Bundesrat together with officials.

Bibliography

Abels, G. and Eppler, A. (2011) 'Auf dem Weg zum 'Mehrebenenparlamentarismus'?, in G. Abels and A. Eppler (eds), *Auf dem Weg zum Mehrebenenparlamentarismus? Funktionen von Parlamenten im Politischen System der EU* (Baden-Baden: Nomos): 17–40.

Arnold, R.D. (1987) 'Political Control of Administrative Officials', *Journal of Law, Economics & Organization*, 3(2): 279–86.

Auel, K. (2007) 'Democratic Accountability and National Parliaments: Redefining the Impact of Parliamentary Scrutiny in EU Affairs', *European Law Journal*, 13(4): 487–504.

——. (2013) *De-Parliamentarisation Re-Considered: 'Representation Without Corresponding Communication', in EU Affairs*, Paper prepared for the 13th EUSA Biennial Conference, Baltimore, 9–11 May 2013.

Auel, K. and Benz, A. (2005) 'The Politics of Adaptation: The Europeanisation of National Parliamentary Systems', *Journal of Legislative Studies*, 11(3–4): 372–93.

Auel, K. and Christiansen, T. (2015) 'After Lisbon: National Parliaments in the European Union', *West European Politics*, 38(2): 261–81.

Auel, K. and Höing, O. (2015) 'National Parliaments and the Eurozone Crisis: Taking Ownership in Difficult Times?', *West European Politics*, 38(2): 375–95.

Auel, K. and Raunio, T. (2014) 'Introduction: Connecting the Electorate? Parliamentary Communication in EU Affairs', *Journal of Legislative Studies*, 20(1): 1–12.

Auel, K., Rozenberg, O. and Tacea, A. (2015a) 'Fighting Back? And, if so, How? Measuring Parliamentary Strength and Activity in EU Affairs', in C. Heffler, C. Neuhold, O. Rozenberg and J. Smith (eds), *The Palgrave Handbook on National Parliaments and the European Union* (London: Palgrave Macmillan): 20–93.

——. (2015b) 'To Scrutinise or Not to Scrutinise? Explaining Variation in EU-Related Activities in National Parliaments', *West European Politics*, 38(2): 282–304.

Auel, K., Rozenberg, O. and Thomas, A. (2012) 'Lost in Transaction? Parliamentary Reserves in EU Bargains', *OPAL Online Paper Series*, 10: 1–30, http://www.pademia.eu/publications/opal-online-paper-series/opal-online-paper-no-102012/.

Barberis, P. (1996) *The Elite of the Elite: Permanent Secretaries in the British Higher Civil Service* (Dartmouth: Dartmouth Publishing Company).

——. (2011) 'The Weberian Legacy', in A. Massey (ed.), *International Handbook on Civil Service Systems* (Cheltenham: Edward Elgar): 13–30.

Barker, A. and Wilson, G.K. (1997) 'Whitehall's Disobedient Servants? Senior Officials' Potential Resistance to Ministers in British Government Departments', *British Journal of Political Science*, 27: 223–46.

Baron, F. (2013) 'Civil Servants: How to Support the Political Level: The French Case', in C. Neuhold, S. Vanhoonacker and L. Verhey (eds), *Civil Servants and Politics* (Basingstoke: Palgrave): 108–23.

Bauer, M. (2009) 'Impact of Administrative Reform of the European Commission: Results from a Survey of Heads of Unit in Policy-making Directorates', *International Review of Administrative Sciences*, 75(3): 459–72.

Bauer, M.W. and Ege, J. (2012) 'Politicization within the European Commission's Bureaucracy', *International Review of Administrative Sciences*, 78(3): 403–24.

Bellamy, R. and Kröger, S. (2013) 'Representation Deficit and Surpluses in EU Policy-making', *Journal of European Integration*, 35(5): 477–97.

——. (2014) 'Domesticating the Democratic Deficit? The Role of National Parliaments and Parties in the EU's System of Governance', *Parliamentary Affairs*, 67(2): 437–57.

Benedetto, G. (2013) 'The EU budget after Lisbon: rigidity and reduced spending?', *Journal of Public Policy*, 33(3): 345–69.

Benz, A. (2007) 'Accountable Multilevel Governance by the Open Method of Coordination?', *European Law Journal*, 13(4): 505–22.

——. (2011) 'Linking Multiple Demoi. Inter-Parliamentary Relations in the EU', *IEV-Online Nr. 1/2011*, Fern Universität in Hagen.

Best, E., Christiansen, T. and Settembri, P. (eds) (2008) *The Institutions of the Enlarged European Union: Continuity and Change* (Cheltenham: Edward Elgar).

Beyers, I. and Dierickx, G. (1998) 'The Working Groups of the Council of the European Union: Supranational or Intergovernmental Negotiations?' *Journal of Common Market Studies*, 36(3): 289–317.

Bijsmans, P. and Altides, C. (2007) '"Bridging the Gap" between EU Politics and Citizens? The European Commission, National Media and EU Affairs in the Public Sphere', *Journal of European Integration*, 29(3): 323–40.

Blischke, Werner (1981) 'Parliamentary Staffs in the German Bundestag', *Legislative Studies Quarterly*, 6(4): 533–58.

Blümel, B. and Neuhold, C. (2001) 'The Parliament of Austria: A Large Potential with Little Implications', in A. Maurer and W. Wessels (eds), *National Parliaments on their Ways to Europe: Losers or Latecomers?* (Baden-Baden: Nomos): 313–36.

Boehmke, F. Gailmard, S. and Patty, J (2005) 'Whose Ear to Bend? Information Sources and Venue Choice in Policy-Making', *Quarterly Journal of Political Science*, 1(2): 139–69.

Bono, G. (2005) 'National Parliaments and EU External Military Operations: Is There any Parliamentary Control?' *European Security*, 14(2): 203–29.

Börzel, T.A. and Risse, T. (2000) 'When Europe Hits Home: Europeanization and Domestic Change', *European Integration online Papers (EIoP)*, 4(15): 1–24.

Brandsma, G. (2012) 'The Effect of Information on Oversight: The European Parliament's Response to Increasing Information on Comitology Decision-making', *International Review of Administrative Sciences*, 78(1): 74–92.

Brandsma, G. and Blom-Hansen, J. (2012) 'Negotiating the Post-Lisbon Comitology System: Institutional Battles Over Delegated Decision-Making', *Journal of Common Market Studies*, 50(6): 939–57.

Burns, C. (2013) 'The European Parliament', in M. Cini and N. Perez-Solorzano Borragan (eds), *European Union Politics*, 4th edition (Oxford: Oxford University Press): 159–72.

Busby, A. (2013) 'Normal Parliament: Exploring the Organisation of Everyday Political Life in an MEP's Office', *Journal of Contemporary European Research*, 9(1): 94–115.

Bußjäger, P. (2010) 'The Austrian Länder: The Relationship of Regional Parliaments to the Executive Power against the Background of Europeanisation', in R. Hrbek (ed.), *Legislatures in Federal Systems and Multi-Level Governance* (Baden-Baden: Nomos): 105–20.

Busuioc, M., Curtin, D. and Groenleer, M. (2011) 'Agency Growth between Autonomy and Accountability: the European Police Office as a "Living Institution" ', *Journal of European Public Policy*, 18(6): 848–67.

Buzogány, A. and Stuchlík, A. (2011) 'Paved with Good Intentions: Ambiguities of Empowering Parliaments after Lisbon', Paper presented at the UACES Conference, *The Lisbon Treaty Evaluated*, London.

CALRE (2011) *Working Group on the Principle of Subsidiarity: Working Plan 2010*, http://archive.scottish.parliament.uk/business/committees/europe/norpec.htm (Accessed 1 December 2012).

Campbell, S. and Laporte, J. (1981) 'The Staff of the Parliamentary Assemblies in France', *Legislative Studies Quarterly*, 6(4): 521–31.

Checkel, J. (2003) ' "Going Native" in Europe? Theorizing Social Interaction in European Institutions', *Comparative Political Studies*, 36(1/2): 209–31.

Christensen, M.B. (2015) 'The Danish Folketing and EU Affairs: Is the Danish Model of Parliamentary Scrutiny Still Best Practice?', in C. Heffler, C. Neuhold, O. Rozenberg and J. Smith (eds), *The Palgrave Handbook on National Parliaments and the European Union* (London: Palgrave Macmillan): 275.

Christiansen, T. (1997) 'Tensions of European Governance: Politicized Bureaucracy and Multiple Accountability in the European Commission', *Journal of European Public Policy*, 4(1): 73–90.

——. (2001) 'Intra-institutional Politics and Inter-Institutional Relations in the EU: Towards Coherent Governance?' *Journal of European Public Policy*, 8(5): 747–69.

——. (2011) 'Administrative Fusion in the European Union: Reviewing a Decade of Comitology Reform', in U. Diedrichs, A. Faber, F. Tekin and G. Umbach (eds), *Europe Reloaded: Differentiation or Fusion?* (Baden-Baden: Nomos): 269–87.

Christiansen, T. and Dobbels, M. (2013) 'Non-Legislative Rule Making after the Lisbon Treaty: Implementing the New System of Comitology and Delegated Acts', *European Law Journal*, 19(1): 42–56.

Christiansen, T., Högenauer, A. and Neuhold, C. (2014) 'National Parliaments in the Post-Lisbon European Union: Bureaucratization rather than Democratization', *Comparative European Politics*, 12(2): 121–40.

Christiansen, T. and Vanhoonacker, S. (2008) 'At a Critical Juncture? Change and Continuity in the Institutional Development of the Council Secretariat', *West European Politics*, 31(4): 751–70.

Cini, M. (1996) *The European Commission: Leadership, Organisation, and Culture in the EU Administration* (Manchester: Manchester University Press).

Clemens, E. and Cook, J. (1999) 'Politics and Institutionalism: Explaining Durability and Change', *Annual Review of Sociology*, 25: 441–66. http://www.jstor.org/stable/223512?seq=1#page_scan_tab_contents.

Coen, D. and Richardson, J. (2009) *Lobbying the European Union: Institutions, Actors, and Issues* (Oxford: Oxford University Press).

Collier, D. (2011) 'Understanding Process-Tracing', *Political Science and Politics*, 44(4): 823–30.

Conference of Speakers (2010) The Stockholm Guidelines for the Conference of Speakers of EU Parliaments, Adopted at the EU Speakers' Conference in Stockholm, Stockholm, 15 May.

Cooper, I. (2006) 'The Watchdogs of Subsidiarity: National Parliaments and the Logic of Arguing in the EU', *Journal of Common Market Studies*, 44(2): 281–304.

——. (2012) 'A "Virtual Third Chamber" for the European Union? National Parliaments after the Treaty of Lisbon', *West European Politics*, 35(3): 441–65.

——. (2013) 'A Yellow Card for the Striker: How National Parliaments Defeated EU Strikes Regulation', 13th EUSA Biennial Conference, 9–11 May 2013, Baltimore.

Corbett, R., Jacobs, F. and Shackleton, M. (2007) *The European Parliament*, 8th edition (London: John Harper Publishing).

——. (2011) *The European Parliament*, 8th edition (London: John Harper Publishing).

COSAC (2011), Rules of Procedure of the Conference of Parliamentary Committees for Union Affairs of Parliaments of the European Union, (2011/C 229/01).

COSAC (2008) *9th Bi-annual Report: Developments in the European Union Procedures and Practices Relevant to Parliamentary Scrutiny*, May 2008, retrieved from: www.cosac.eu/documents/bi-annual-reports-of-cosac/ (Accessed 15 December 2013).

—— (2013a) *History of COSAC* (Brussels: COSAC Secretariat), retrieved from: http://www.cosac.eu/documents/.

—— (2013b) *Twentieth Bi-annual Report: Developments in European Union Procedures and Practices Relevant to Parliamentary Scrutiny* (Brussels: COSAC Secretariat).

Costa, O. and Latek, M. (2001) 'Paradoxes and Limits of Interparliamentary Cooperation in the European Union', *Journal of European Integration*, 23(2): 139–64.

Crum, B. (2013) 'Saving the Euro at the Cost of Democracy?' *JCMS: Journal of Common Market Studies*, 51(4): 614–30.

Crum, B. and Fossum, J. E. (2009) 'The Multilevel Parliamentary Field: A Framework for Theorizing Representative Democracy in the EU', *European Political Science Review*, 1(2): 249–71.

——. (2013) 'Practices of Interparliamentary Coordination in International Politics: The European Union and Beyond', in B. Crum and J.E Fossum (eds), *Practices of Inter-Parliamentary Coordination in International Politics: The European Union and Beyond* (Colchester: ECPR Press): 1–16.

Curtin, D. (2007) 'Holding (Quasi-)Autonomous EU Administrative Actors to Public Account', *European Law Journal*, 13(4): 523–41.

Curtin, D. and Egeberg, M. (2008) 'Tradition and Innovation: Europe's Accumulated Executive Order', *West European Politics*, 31(4): 639–61.

Cygan, A. (2013) *Accountability, Parliamentarism and Transparency in the EU: The Role of National Parliaments* (Cheltenham: Edward Elgar).

De Ruiter, R. (2010) 'EU Soft Law and the Functioning of Representative Democracy: The Use of Methods of Open Coordination by Dutch and British Parliamentarians', *Journal of European Public Policy*, 17(6): 874–90.

——. (2014) 'Public Parliamentary Activities and Open Methods of Coordination', *The Journal of Legislative Studies*, 20(1): 62–77.

De Ruiter, R. and Neuhold, C. (2012a) 'The Winner Takes It All? The Implications of the Lisbon Treaty for the EPs Legislative Rile in Co-decision', In F. Laursen (ed.), *The Lisbon Treaty: institutional choices and implementation,* (Farnham:Ashgate Publishing Ltd): 103–18.

De Ruiter, R. and Neuhold, C. (2012b) 'Why Is Fast Track the Way to Go? Justifications for Early Agreement in the Co-decision Procedure and their Effects', *European Law Journal*, 18(5): 536–54.

De Wilde, P. (2012) *Why the Early Warning Mechanism Does Not Alleviate the Democratic Deficit* OPAL Online Paper 6: 23, http://www.pademia.eu/publications/opal-online-paper-series/opal-online-paper-no-62012/.

De Wilde, P. and Trenz, H.-J. (2012) 'Denouncing European Integration: Euroscepticism as Polity Contestation', *European Journal of Social Theory*, 15(4): 537–54.

DeGregorio, C. (1994) 'Professional Committee Staff as Policy Making Partners in the US Congress', *Congress & The Presidency*, 21(1): 49.

Dehousse, R. and Thompson, A. (2012) 'Intergovernmentalists in the Commission: Foxes in the Henhouse?' *Journal of European Integration*, 34(2): 113–32.

Delreux, T. and Randour, F. (2015) 'Belgium: Institutional and Administrative Adaptation but Limited Political Interest', in C. Heffler, C. Neuhold, O. Rozenberg and J. Smith (eds), *The Palgrave Handbook on National Parliaments and the European Union* (London: Palgrave Macmillan), 153–69.

Deubner, C. (2013) *The Difficult Role of Parliaments in the Reformed Governance of the European Economic and Monetary Union*, Study No.19, Foundation for European Progressive Studies, Brussels.

Deutscher Bundestag (2013) www.bundestag.de/bundestag/abgeordnete17/mdb_diaeten/1334d.html (Accessed 13 December 2012).

Dimier, V. and Mcgeever, M. (2006) 'Diplomats Without a Flag: The Institutionalization of the Delegations of the Commission in African, Caribbean and Pacific Countries*', *JCMS: Journal of Common Market Studies*, 44(3): 483–505.

Dobbels, M. and Neuhold, C. (2013) '"The Roles Bureaucrats Play": The Input of the European Parliament (EP) Administrators into the Ordinary Legislative Procedure: A Case Study Approach', *Journal of European Integration*, 35(4): 375–90.

——. (2014) 'Who Selects What and How? How the European Parliament Obtains and Processes Information for Policy-Making', in T. Blom, and S. Vanhoonacker (2014) *The Politics of Information. The Case of the European Union* (London: Palgrave): 78–92.

——. (2015) 'Officials "Pre-Cooking" EU Affairs? The Role of EP Officials in the Ordinary Legislative Procedure (OLP)', in M. Bauer and J. Trondal (eds), *The Palgrave Handbook of the European Administrative System* (London: Palgrave): 246–62.

Domorenok, E. (2009) 'The Committee of the Regions: In Search of Identity', *Regional and Federal Studies*, 19(1): 143–63.

Duke, S. (2009) 'Providing for European-Level Diplomacy after Lisbon: The Case of the European External Action Service', *Hague Journal of Diplomacy*, 4(2): 211–33.

——. (2012) 'Now We Are One... A Rough Start for the EEAS', *EIPAScope*, 1: 25–29.

Egeberg, M. (1995) 'Bureaucrats as Public Policy-Makers and Their Self-interest', *Journal of Theoretical Politics*, 7(2): 157–67.

Egeberg, M., Gornitzka, A. and Trondal, J. (2014) 'People Who Run the European Parliament: Staff Demography and Its Implications', *Journal of European Integration*, 36(7): 659–75.

Egeberg, M., Gornitzka, A., Trondal, J. and Johannessen, M. (2013) 'Parliament Staff: Unpacking the Behaviour of Officials in the European Parliament', *Journal of European Public Policy*, 20(4): 495–514.

Ehin, P. (2015) 'The Estonian Parliament and EU affairs: A Watchdog that does not Bark?', in C. Heffler, C. Neuhold, O. Rozenberg and J. Smith (eds), *The Palgrave Handbook on National Parliaments and the European Union* (London: Palgrave Macmillan): 513–30.

Eppler, A. (2014) 'Interparliamentary Relations: New Deliberative Space or Instrument to Improve Parliamentary Control?', 21st International Conference of Europeanists, Washington, DC, 14–16 March 2014.

Eurofond (2012) Working Time, http://www.eurofond.europa.eu/industrialrelations/dictionary/definitions/WORKINGTIME.htm.

European Commission. (2008) 'Proposal for a Regulation of the European Parliament and of the Council on Novel Foods and amending Regulation (EC) No 257/97', COM(2007) 872 final,14 January 2008.

——. (2009) 'Proposal for a Council Regulation Establishing a Multi-annual Plan for the Western Stock of Atlantic Horse Mackerel and the Fisheries Exploiting That Stock', 2009/0057 (CNS).

European Communities (2004) 'Staff Regulations of Officials of the European Communities' (Brussels: Commission of the European Communities), retrieved from: http://ec.europa.eu/dgs/personnel_administration/statut/tocen100.pdf.

European Parliament. (2011) Rules of Procedure of the Conference of Parliamentary Committees for Union Affairs of Parliaments of the European Union (2011/C 229/01).

——. (2014) The European Union's General Budget for the Financial Year 2014 (2014/67/EU, Euratom).

Figulova, A. (2015) 'The Slovak Parliament and EU Affairs – In Need of a Wake-up Call', in C. Heffler, C. Neuhold, O. Rozenberg and J. Smith (eds), *The Palgrave Handbook on National Parliaments and the European Union* (London: Palgrave Macmillan): 632–48.

Fleischer, J. (2014) 'More Scrutiny, More Harmony? The Early Warning System and Executive-Legislative Relations at Subnational Level?', 21st International Conference of Europeanists, Washington, DC, 14–16 March 2014.

Gailmard, S. and Patty, J.W. (2007) 'Slackers and Zealots: Civil Service, Policy Discretion, and Bureaucratic Expertise', *American Journal of Political Science*, 51(4): 873–89.

Gattermann, K. and Hefftler, C. (2015) 'Beyond Institutional Capacity: Political Motivation and Parliamentary Behaviour in the Early Warning System', *West European Politics*, 38(2): 305–34.

Gattermann, K., Högenauer, A.L. and Huff, A. (2013) 'National Parliaments after Lisbon: Towards Mainstreaming of EU Affairs?', *OPAL Online Paper* No. 13/2013, http://opal-europe.org/index.php?option=com_content&view=article&id=95 (Accessed 23 December 2015).

——. (2015) 'Research Note: Studying a New Phase of Europeanization of National Parliaments', *European Political Science*.

Goetz, K.H. (2011) 'The Development and Current Features of the German Civil Service System', in H.A.G.M. Bekke and F.M. van der Meer (eds.), *Civil Service Systems in Western Europe* (Cheltenham: Edward Elgar): 37–66.

Goetz, K.H. and Meyer-Sahling, J.-H. (2008) 'The Europeanisation of National Political Systems: Parliaments and Executives', *Living Reviews in European Governance*, 3(2): 1–30.

Gornitzka, Å. and Sverdrup, U. (2008) 'Who Consults? The Configuration of Expert Groups in the European Union', *West European Politics*, 31(4): 725–50.

Graziano, P. and Vink, M. (2008) *Europeanization – New Research Agendas*, London: Palgrave Macmillan.

Greer, S.L. and Jarman, H. (2011) 'The British Civil Service System', in H.A.G.M. Bekke and F.M. van der Meer (eds), *Civil Service Systems in Western Europe* (Cheltenham: Edward Elgar): 13–35.

Groen, A. and Christiansen, T. (2015) 'National Parliaments in the European Union: Conceptual Choices in the European Union's Constitutional Debate', in C. Hefftler, C. Neuhold, O. Rozenberg and J. Smith (eds), *The Palgrave Handbook of National Parliaments and the European Union* (London: Palgrave Macmillan), 43–59.

Groenleer, M. (2009) *The Autonomy of European Union Agencies: A Comparative Study of Institutional Development* (Delft: Eburon Uitgeverij B.V).

Groenleer, M.L.P. and Van Schaik, L.G. (2007) 'United we Stand? The European Union's International Actorness in the Cases of the International Criminal Court and the Kyoto Protocol', *Journal of Common Market Studies*, 45(5): 969–98.

Grossman, S. and Hart, D. (1983) 'An Analysis of the Principal Agent Problem', *Econometrica*, 50(1): 7–46.

Haas, P. (1992) 'Introduction: Epistemic Communities and International Policy Coordination', *International Organization*, 46(1): 1–35.

Hammond, T. (1986) 'Agenda Control, Organisational Structures and Bureaucratic Politics', *American Journal of Political Science*, 30(2): 379–420.

Harfst, P. and Schnapp, K. (2003) 'Instrumente parlamentarischer Kontrolle der Exekutive in westlichen Demokratien', *Discussion Paper SP IV 2003–201*, Wissenschaftszentrum Berlin für Sozialforschung (WZB).

Häsing, J. and Buzogany, A. (2013) 'Europäisierung des Deutschen Landesparlamentarismus? Die Rolle der Landtagsverwaltungen bei der Umsetzung der Subsidiaritätskontrolle', Paper presented at the conference on *Politik, Region(en) und Kultur in der vergleichenden Politikwissenschaft*,Leipzig, 9–11 October 2013.

Hasters, L. (2014) 'The COSAC Secretariat: Tasks and Function', Paper written for Research Master European Studies.

Hefftler, C. (2015) 'An Ever Closer Inter-parliamentary Network? National Parliaments' Priorities in Inter-parliamentary Cooperation in the EU', Paper presented at EUSA Conference, Boston, 5 March 2015.

Hefftler, C. and Gattermann, K. (2015) 'Interparliamentary Cooperation in the European Union: Patterns, Problems and Potential', in C. Hefftler, C. Neuhold, O. Rozenberg and J. Smith (eds), *The Palgrave Handbook of National Parliaments and the European Union* (London: Palgrave Macmillan): 94–115.

Hefftler, C., Neuhold, C. Rozenberg, O. and Smith, J (2015) (eds), *The Palgrave Handbook of National Parliaments and the European Union* (London: Palgrave Macmillan).

Hegeland, H. (2015) 'The Swedish Parliament and EU Affairs: From Reluctant Player to Europeanized Actor', in C. Heffler, C. Neuhold, O. Rozenberg and J. Smith (eds), *The Palgrave Handbook on National Parliaments and the European Union* (London: Palgrave Macmillan), 425–41.

Herranz-Surrallés, A. (2014) 'The EU's Multilevel Parliamentary (Battle)Field: Inter-parliamentary Cooperation and Conflict in Foreign and Security Policy', *West European Politics*, 37(5): 957–75.

Hix, S. (1999) 'Dimensions and Alignments in European Union Politics: Cognitive Constraints and Partisan Responses', *European Journal of Political Research*, 35(1): 69–106.

Hix, S. and Høyland, B. (2013) 'Empowerment of the European Parliament', *Annual Review of Political Science*, 16: 171–89.

Hodson, D. (2015) 'De Novo Bodies and the New Intergovernmentalism – The Case of the European Central Bank', in C.J. Bickerton, D. Hodson and U. Puetter (eds), *The New Intergovernmentalism: States and Supranational Actors in the Post-Maastricht Era* (Oxford: Oxford University Press): 263–88.

Högenauer, A.L. 2016 (in press) 'The Scottish Parliament – An Active Player in a Multi-level European Union?', in G. Abels and A. Eppler (eds), *Subnational Parliaments in an EU Multi-level Parliamentary System: Taking Stock of the Post-Lisbon Era*, Foster Europe International Studies Series, vol. 3 (New Jersey: Studienverlag Innsbruck and Transaction Publishers): 247–63.

——. (2014) 'The Limits of Territorial Interest Representation in the European Union', *Territory, Politics, Governance*, DOI:10.1080/21622671.2014.911701, 3 June 2014.

——. (2015) 'The Dutch Parliament and EU Affairs: Decentralizing Scrutiny', in C. Heffler, C. Neuhold, O. Rozenberg and J. Smith (eds), *The Palgrave Handbook on National Parliaments and the European Union* (London: Palgrave Macmillan): 252–71.

Högenauer, A.-L. and Christiansen, T. (2015) 'Parliamentary Administrations in the Scrutiny of EU Decision-making', in C. Hefftler, C. Neuhold, O. Rozenberg and J. Smith (eds), *The Palgrave Handbook of National Parliaments and the European Union* (London: Palgrave Macmillan): 116–32.

Högenauer, A. and Neuhold, C. (2013) 'National Parliaments after Lisbon: Administrations on the Rise?', *OPAL Online Paper* No. 12/2013, http://www.opal-europe.org/index.php?option=com_content&view=article&id=92 (Accessed 15 August 2013).

——. (2015) 'National Parliaments after Lisbon: Administrations on the Rise?', *West European Politics*, 38(2): 335–54.

Höing, O. (2015) 'With a Little Help from the Constitutional Court. The Bundestag on Its Way to an Active Policy-shaper', in C. Heffler, C. Neuhold, O. Rozenberg and J. Smith, *The Palgrave Handbook on National Parliaments and the European Union* (London: Palgrave Macmillan): 191–208.

Holzhacker, R. (2005) 'The Power of Opposition Parliamentary Groups in European Scrutiny', *Journal of Legislative Studies*, 11(3–4): 428–45.

Hooghe, L. (2001) *The European Commission and the Integration of Europe: Images of Governance* (Cambridge: Cambridge University Press).

House of Lords, European Union Committee (2014) *The Role of National Parliaments in the European Union*, 9th report of Session 2013–14, HL Paper 151, 24 March 2014.

Hrabálek, M. and Strelkov, A. (2015) 'The Czech Parliament and European Integration', in C. Heffler, C. Neuhold, O. Rozenberg and J. Smith (eds), *The Palgrave Handbook on National Parliaments and the European Union* (London: Palgrave Macmillan): 494–512.

Hrbek, R. (2010) 'Parliaments in EU Multi-level Governance', in R. Hrbek (ed.), *Legislatures in Federal Systems and Multi-Level Governance* (Nomos: Baden-Baden): 36–150.

Huber, J. (2000) 'Delegation to Civil Servants in Parliamentary Democracies', *European Journal of Political Research*, 37: 397–413.

Huber, J.D. and McCarty, N. (2004) 'Bureaucratic Capacity, Delegation, and Reform', *American Political Science Review*, 98(3): 481–94.

Huff, A. (2015) 'Executive Privilege Reaffirmed? Parliamentary Scrutiny of the CFSP and CSDP', *West European Politics*, 38(2): 396–415.

Ilonszki, G. (2015) 'The Hungarian Parliament and EU Affairs: A Modest Actor Dominated by the Executive', in C. Heffler, C. Neuhold, O. Rozenberg and J. Smith, *The Palgrave Handbook on National Parliaments and the European Union* (London: Palgrave Macmillan): 531–47.

Jančić, D. (2015) 'The Portuguese Parliament and EU Affairs: From Inert to Agile Democratic Control', in C. Heffler, C. Neuhold, O. Rozenberg, J. Smith, *The Palgrave Handbook on National Parliaments and the European Union* (London: Palgrave Macmillan): 366–86.

Judge, D. (1995) 'The Failure of National Parliaments?', *West European Politics*, 18(3): 79–100.

Juncos, A. and Pomorska, K. (2011) 'Invisible and Unaccountable? National Representatives and Council Officials in EU Foreign Policy', *Journal of European Public Policy*, 18(8): 1096–14.

Kaczynski, P. M. (2011) *Paper Tigers or Sleeping Beauties? National Parliaments in the Post-Lisbon European Political System*, CEPS Special Report, Brussels.

Kasack, C. (2004) 'The Legislative Impact of the European Parliament Under the Revised Co-decision Procedure: Environmental, Public Health and Consumer Protection Policies', *European Union Politics*, 5: 241–60.

Kassim, H. and Menon, A. (2003) 'The Principal–Agent Approach and the Study of the European Union: Promise Unfulfilled?', *Journal of European Public Policy*, 10(1): 121–39.

Kassim, H., Peterson, J., Bauer, M.W., Connolly, S., Dehousse, R., Hooghe, L. and Thompson, A. (2013) *The European Commission of the Twenty-First Century* (Oxford: Oxford University Press).

Kiiver, P. (2006) *The National Parliaments in the European Union: A Critical View on EU Constitution-Building* (The Hague: Kluwer Law International).

——. (2011) 'The Early-Warning System for the Principle of Subsidiarity: The National Parliament as a Conseil d'Etat for Europe', *European Law Review*, 36: 98–108.

——. (2012) *The Early Warning System for the Principle of Subsidiarity. Constitutional Theory and Empirical Reality* (London and New York: Routledge).

Lammert, N. (2009) 'Europa der Bürger – Parlamentarische Perspektiven der Union nach dem Lissabon-Vertrag', Speech at the Humboldt University, 1 December 2009.

Linn, S. and Sobolewski, F. (2012) *So arbeitet der Deutsche Bundestag*, 17. Wahlperiode, 25th edition (Rheinbreitbach: NDV Neue Darmstädter Verlagsanstalt).

Mahoney, H. (2010) 'European Council Seen as Winner under Lisbon Treaty', *EU Observer*, 27 May 2010.

Manley, J.F. (1968) 'Congressional Staff and Public Policy-Making: The Joint Committee on International Revenue Taxation', *Journal of Politics*, 30(4): 1046–67.

Marshall, D. (2012) 'Do Rapporteurs Receive Independent Expert Policy Advice? Indirect Lobbying via the European Parliament's Committee Secretariat', *Journal of European Public Policy*, 19(9), 1377–95.

Mastenbroek, E., Zwaan, P., Groen, A., Meurs, W., Reiding, H., Dörrenbächer, N. and Neuhold, C. (2014) 'Engaging with Europe. Evaluating National Parliamentary Control of EU Decision Making after the Lisbon Treaty', Report prepared for the Dutch Tweede Kamer.

Maurer, A. and Wessels, W. (eds) (2001) *National Parliaments on their Ways to Europe. Losers or Latecomers?* (Baden-Baden: Nomos Verlag).

McCubbins, M., Noll, R. and Weingast, B. (1987) 'Administrative Procedures as Instruments of Political Control', *Journal of Law, Economics, and Organization*, 3(2): 243–77.

McCubbins, M.D. and Page, T. (1987) 'A Theory of Congressional Delegation', in M.D. McCubbins and T. Sullivan (eds), *Congress: Structure and Policy* (Cambridge: Cambridge University Press): 409–25.

McCubbins, M.D. and Schwartz, T. (1984) 'Congressional Oversight Overlooked: Police Patrols Versus Fire Alarms', *American Journal of Political Science*, 28(1): 165–79.

Meller, N. (1952) 'The Policy Position of Legislative Service Agencies', *Western Political Quarterly*, 5(1): 109–23.

Miklin, E. (2015) 'The Austrian Parliament and EU affairs: Gradually Living up to Its Legal Potential', in C. Heffler, C. Neuhold, O. Rozenberg, J. Smith (eds), *The Palgrave Handbook on National Parliaments and the European Union* (London: Palgrave Macmillan): 389–405.

Moe, T.M. (1984) 'The New Economics of Organization', *American Journal of Political Science*, 28: 739–77.

——. (1987) 'An Assessment of the Positive Theory of Congressional Dominance', *Legislative Studies Quarterly*, 12(11): 475–520.

Moravcsik, A. (1995) 'Why International Cooperation Strengthens National Executives: The Case of the European Community', Paper presented at the 1995 ECSA Conference, Charleston, SC.

Naômé, C. (2008) 'EU Enlargement and the European Court of Justice', in E. Best, T. Christiansen and P. Settembri (eds) *The Institutions of the Enlarged European Union: Continuity and Change* (Cheltenham: Edward Elgar): 100–19.

Neuhold, C. and Dobbels, M. (2014) 'Paper-keepers or Policy-shapers? The Conditions under which EP Officials Impact on the EU Policy-process', *Comparative European Politics*, doi: 10.1057/cep.2014.7

Neuhold, C. and Högenauer, A.L. (2013) 'Administrators Networking EU Affairs? The Role of Parliamentary Officials in Inter-parliamentary Coordination and Control', 13th EUSA Biennial Conference, Baltimore, 9–11 May 2013.

Neuhold, C. and Smith, J. (2015) 'Conclusion', in C. Heffler, C. Neuhold, O. Rozenberg and J. Smith (eds), *The Palgrave Handbook on National Parliaments and the European Union* (London: Palgrave Macmillan): 668–86.

Neunreither, K. (2006) 'Elected Legislators and their Unelected Assistants in the European Parliament', *Journal of Legislative Studies*, 8(4): 40–60

Norton, P. (ed.) (1996) *National Parliaments and the European Union* (London: Routledge).

O'Brennan, J. and Raunio, T. (2007) 'Introduction. Deparliamentarization and European Integration', in J. O'Brennan and T. Raunio (eds), *National Parliaments within the Enlarged European Union. From 'Victims' of Integration to Competitive Actors?* (London: Routledge): 1–26.

——. (eds) (2007) *National Parliaments within the Enlarged European Union: From 'Victims' of Integration to Competitive Actors?* (Abingdon: Routledge).

Olsen, J. (2006) 'Maybe It Is Time to Rediscover Bureaucracy', *Journal of Public Administration Research and Theory*, 16(1): 1–2.

Ontwerp van samenwerkingsakkoord betreffende de uitoefening van de bevoegdheden aan de nationale parlementen toegekend in het verdrag van Lissabon, 7 and 9 July 2008.

Page, E. and Jenkins, B. (2005) *Policy Bureaucracy: Government with a Cast of Thousands* (Oxford: Oxford University Press).

Patterson, Samuel C. (1970) 'The Political Staffs of Congressional Committees', *Administrative Science Quarterly*, 25(1):22–38.

Pegan, A. (2015) *An Analysis of Legislative Assistance in the European Parliament*, Dissertation, presented on 27 March 2015 in Luxembourg: Luxembourg.

Pegan, A. and Högenauer, A.L. (in press) 'The Role of Parliamentary Administrations in Interparliamentary Cooperation', in N. Lupo and C. Fasone (eds), *Interparliamentary Cooperation in the Composite European Constitution* (London: Hart Publishing).

Perez, S. (2007) 'Parlament et administration de l'Union européenne', in *Annuaire européen d'administration publique*, Tome 29, Parlement et administration en Europe, PU Aix-Marseille.

Peters, D., Wagner, W. and Deitelhoff, N. (2010) 'Parliaments and European Security Policy: Mapping the Parliamentary Field', *EIOP European Integration Online Papers* 14 (Special Issue 1): 1–25.

Peters, G. (1998) *Comparative Politics – Theory and Methods* (New York: New York University Press).

Peterson, J. (2011) 'The Santer Era: The European Commission in Normative, Historical and Theoretical Perspective', *Journal of European Public Policy*, 6(1): 46–65.

Petitjean, S. (2012) 'Commission Withdraws Monti II Proposal', in *Europolitics*, http://www.europolitics.info/social/commission-withdraws-monti-ii-proposal-art342821-25.html, 13 September.

Pinheiro, B. (2012) 'O Tratado de Lisboa e a adaptação dos parlamentos nacionais aos desafios da integração europeia: o caso dos representantes permanentes dos Parlamentos junto das instituições da União Europeia' https://www.repository.utl.pt/handle/10400.5/5124.

President of the Portuguese Parliament (2008) *Concerning the Statute of the Permanent Representative of the Portuguese Parliament (Antenna) to the European Union*, Order no. 195/X, São Bento Palace, 24 June.

Provan, J. (2001) 'Legislative Assistance to Members – A Rethink,' Working Document No. 6 on Internal Reform.

Rasmussen, A. and Reh, C. (2013) 'The Consequences of Concluding Codecision Early: Trilogues and Intra-institutional Bargaining Success', *Special Issue of the Journal of European Public Policy*, 20(7): 1006–24.

Raunio, T. (2002) 'Why European Integration Increases Leadership Autonomy within Political Parties', *Party Politics*, 8(4): 405–22.

——. (2007) 'National Legislatures and the Constitutional Treaty', in J. O'Brennan and T. Raunio (eds), *National Parliaments within the Enlarged European Union: From 'Victims' of Integration to Competitive Actors?* (Abingdon: Routledge): 79–92.

——. (2010) 'Destined for Irrelevance? Subsidiarity Control by National Parliaments', *Europe Working Article*, 2010(36), Real Instituto Elcano.

——. (2011) 'The Gatekeepers of European Integration? The Functions of National Parliaments in the EU Political System', *Journal of European Integration*, 33(3): 303–21.

——. (2015) 'The Finnish Eduskunta and EU: The Strengths and Weaknesses of a Mandating System', in C. Heffler, C. Neuhold, O. Rozenberg and J. Smith (eds), *The Palgrave Handbook on National Parliaments and the European Union* (London: Palgrave Macmillan): 406–24.

Raunio, T. and Wright, A. (2006) 'Holyrood and Europe: An Incremental Response to Deparliamentarization', *Regional and Federal Studies*, 16(3): 281–96.

Règlement du Parlement de la communauté francophone, 13 July 2013

Reh, C. (2007) 'Pre-cooking the European Constitution? The Role of Government Representatives in EU Reform', *Journal of European Public Policy*, 14(8): 1186–07.

Richardson, J. (2006) 'Policy-making in the EU. Interests, Ideas and Garbage Cans of Primeval Soup,' in J. Richardson (ed.), *European Union: Power and Policy-making* (London: Routledge): 3–30.

Ripoll Servent, A. (2014) 'The Role of the European Parliament in International Negotiations after Lisbon', *Journal of European Public Policy*, 21(4): 568–86.

Ripoll Servent, A. and MacKenzie, A. (2012) 'The European Parliament as a "Norm Taker"? EU-US Relations after the SWIFT Agreement', *European Foreign Affairs Review*, 17(2.1): 71–86.

Rittberger, B. (2010) 'Multi-level Governance and Parliaments in the European Union', in H. Enderlein, S. Wälti and M. Zürn (eds), *Handbook on Multi-level Governance* (Cheltenham: Edward Elgar): 239–52.

Rittberger, B. and Wonka, A. (2013) *Agency Governance in the EU* (London: Routledge).

Romanyshyn, I. and Neuhold, C. (2011) 'The European Parliament's Administration: Between Neutral and Politicised Competence', in C. Neuhold, and S. Vanhoonacker, and L. Verhey (eds), *Civil Servants and Politics* (London: Palgrave): 205–28.

Ross, G. (1995) *Jacques Delors and European Integration*, Oxford University Press, USA.

Rothenberger, S. and Vogt, O. (2007) 'The "Orange Card": A Fitting Response to National Parliaments' Marginalisation in EU Decision-Making?', Paper presented at the *Stiftung Wissenschaft und Politik Conference*, Berlin, 13 June.

Ryle, M.T. (1981) 'The Legislative Staff of the British House of Commons', *Legislative Studies Quarterly*, 6(4): 497–519.

Schäfer, A. (2013) 'Deutscher Bundestag', 232. Plenary Session Berlin, 29070–71.

Shackleton, M. and Raunio, T. (2003) 'Codecision since Amsterdam: a laboratory for institutional innovation and change', *Journal of European Public Policy*, 10(2): 171–88.

Shapiro, M. (1997) 'The Problems of Independent Agencies in the United States and the European Union', *Journal of European Public Policy*, 4(2): 276–77.
Sotiropoulos, D.A. (2015) 'The Greek Parliament and the European Union After the Lisbon Treaty: A Missed Opportunity to Empower Parliament', in C. Heffler, C. Neuhold, O. Rozenberg and J. Smith (eds), *The Palgrave Handbook on National Parliaments and the European Union* (London: Palgrave Macmillan): 335–47.
Spreitzer, A. (2013) *Administrating EU affairs in the Luxembourgish Parliament*, Paper presented at the ECPR conference, Bordeaux, 4 September 2013.
Sprungk, C. (2011) 'Parlamentarismus im Europäischen Mehrebenensystem. Zum Wandel von Rollenanforderungen an Nationale Parlamente in EU Angelegenheiten', in G. Abels and A. Eppler (eds), *Auf dem Weg zum Mehrebenenparlamentarismus? Funktionen von Parlamenten im Politischen System der EU* (Baden-Baden: Nomos): 211–26.
Stahl, G. (2009) 'Die Rolle des AdR bei der regional Interessenvertretung', in K.-H. Lambertz and M. Große Hüttmann (eds), *Europapolitik und Europafähigkeit von Regionen* (Nomos: Baden-Baden): 136–40.
Stavridis, S. (2014) *The New Inter-Parliamentary Conference on the CFSP/CSDP* (Miami: Miami-Florida European Union Center of Excellence).
Strelkov, A. (2015) 'Making Sense of the New "Opportunity Structure": Parliamentary Actors in the Aftermath of the Lisbon Treaty', *West European Politics*, 38(2): 355–74.
Sturm, R. and Zimmermann-Steinhart, P. (2005) *Föderalismus. Eine Einführung.* (Baden-Baden: Nomos).
Szalay, K. (2005) 'Scrutiny of EU Affairs in the National Parliaments of the New Member States: Comparative Analysis', Hungarian National Assembly: Budapest.
Tordoff, L. (2000) 'The Conference of European Affairs Committees: A Collective Voice for National Parliaments in the European Union', *Journal of Legislative Studies*, 6(4): 1–8.
Trondal, J., Van Den Berg, C. and Suvarierol, S. (2008) 'The Compound Machinery of Government: The Case of Seconded Officials in the European Commission', *Governance* 21(2): 253–274.
Tweede Kamer (2011) 'Organogram EU-Staf Tweede Kamer', retrieved from: http://www.cosac.eu/staff-structures/ (Accessed 15 February 2013).
Van der Meer, F. and Dijkstra, G.S.A. (2011) 'Civil Service Systems in Western Europe: Variations and Similarities', in H. Bekke and F. Van Der Meer (eds), *Civil Service Systems in Western Europe* (Cheltenham: Edward Elgar): 271–86.
Vanhoonacker, S. and Verhey, L. (eds) (2013) *Civil Servants and Politics* (London: Palgrave Macmillan).
Vara Arribas, G. and Bourdin, D. (2011) *The Role of Regional Parliaments in the Process of Subsidiarity Analysis within the Early Warning System of the Lisbon Treaty*, Study commissioned by the Committee of the Regions, DOI: 10.2863/35536.
Vara Arribas, G. and Högenauer, A.L. (2015) 'Legislative Regions after Lisbon: A New Role for Regional Assemblies?', in C. Heffler, C. Neuhold, O. Rozenberg and J. Smith (eds), *The Palgrave Handbook on National Parliaments and the European Union* (London: Palgrave Macmillan): 133–49.
Vehar, P. (2007) 'The National Assembly of the Republic of Slovenia and EU Affairs before and after Accession', in J. O'Brennan and T. Raunio (eds), *National*

Parliaments within the Enlarged European Union: From 'Victims' of Integration to Competitive Actors? (Abingdon: Routledge): 241–55.

Weber, M. ([1922] 1978) in G. Roth and C. Wittich (eds), *Economy and Society: An Outline of Interpretative Sociology* (Berkeley, CA: University of California Press).

Weber-Panariello, P.A. (1995) *Nationale Parlamente in der Europäischen Union* (Baden-Baden: Nomos).

Wendler, F. (2014) 'Debating Europe in National Parliaments Justification and Political Polarization in Debates on the EU in Austria, France, Germany and the United Kingdom', *OPAL Online Paper*, 17, 2014.

Wessels, W. (1998) 'Comitology: Fusion in Action. Politico-administrative Trends in the EU System', *Journal of European Public Policy*, 5(2): 209–34.

Wille, A.C. (2010) 'Political-Bureaucratic Accountability in the EU Commission: Modernising the Executive', *West European Politics*, 33(5): 1093–116.

Winzen, T. (2011) 'Technical or Political? An Exploration of the Work of Officials in the Committees of the European Parliament', *Journal of Legislative Studies*, 17(1): 27–44.

——. (2014) 'Bureaucracy and Democracy: Intra-Parliamentary Delegation in European Union Affairs', *Journal of European Integration*, 36(7): 677–95.

Winzen, T., Roederer-Rynning, C. and Schimmelfennig, F. (2012) 'Five Decades of Parliamentarization: The Evolution of the EU' s Multi-level Parliamentary System', ECPR Standing Groups on Parliaments (Dublin): 1–19.

Wlezien C. (2005) 'On the Salience of Political Issues: The Problem with "Most Important Problem" ', *Electoral Studies*, 24(4): 555–79.

www.bundestag.de/bundestag/abgeordnete18/mdb_diaeten/index.html (Accessed 24 February 2013).

www.opal-europe.org, Country Reports.

Index

Note: The letters 'f', and 't' following locators refer to figures and tables respectively.

CPI Antony Rowe
Chippenham, UK
2016-12-09 21:20